Finding God In The Verbs

Crafting A Fresh Language Of Prayer

Jennie Isbell
J. Brent Bill

16

EasyRead Large

ISBN: 9781459695597

RHYW

Copyright Page from the Original Book

InterVarsity Press
P.O. Box 1400, Downers Grove, IL 60515-1426
ivpress.com
email@ivpress.com

InterVarsity Press® is the book-publishing division of InterVarsity Christian Fellowship/USA®, a movement of students and faculty active on campus at hundreds of universities, colleges and schools of nursing in the United States of America, and a member movement of the International Fellowship of Evangelical Students. For information about local and regional activities, visit intervarsity.org.

All Scripture quotations, unless otherwise indicated, are taken from THE HOLY BIBLE, NEW INTERNATIONAL VERSION®, NIV® *Copyright © 1973, 1978, 1984, 2011 by Biblica, Inc.™ Used by permission. All rights reserved worldwide.*

While any stories in this book are true, some names and identifying information may have been changed to protect the privacy of individuals.

"Church Register" copyright "The Sacred Sandwich" http://sacredsandwich.com/archives/9273. Used with permission.

"Thank You, Good Night" by Carrie Newcomer, copyright 2013 Windchime Productions. Used with permission.

Cover design: Cindy Kiple
Interior design: Beth McGill
Images: © ru3apr/iStockphoto

ISBN 978-0-8308-3596-6 (print)
ISBN 978-0-8308-9718-6 (digital)

Printed in the United States of America ∞

Library of Congress Cataloging-in-Publication Data
Isbell, Jennifer L.
  Finding God in the verbs : crafting a fresh language of prayer /
Jennie Isbell and J. Brent Bill.
      pages cm
  Includes bibliographical references.
  ISBN 978-0-8308-3596-6 (pbk. : alk. paper)
  1. Prayer—Christianity. 2. Spiritual exercises. I. Title.
  BV215.I83 2015
  248.3'2—dc23
2014044447

P	21	20	19	18	17	16	15	14	13	12	11	10	9	8	7	6	5	4	3	2	1
Y	33	32	31	30	29	28	27	26	25	24	23	22	21	20	19	18	17	16	15

TABLE OF CONTENTS

Praise for Finding God in the Verbs

"In this thoughtful, discerning book, Jennie Isbell and Brent Bill invite readers into a closer engagement with prayer by means of a closer engagement with language itself. Using humor, personal experience and deep understanding, the authors lead us into an exploration of prayer that is courageous and profound. This book merits a place on every bookshelf devoted to the life of prayer."

Erin McGraw, author of *The Good Life*

"This exciting book, full of fresh ideas, is an invitation to discovery of self and to theological growth through prayer. It is tinged with humor and filled with stories, summoning the reader to dance, to see with new eyes and to experience the fullness of embodiment. Jennie Isbell and Brent Bill remind us that prayer is about desire and cultivating awareness."

Michael Birkel, professor of religion, Earlham College

"*Finding God in the Verbs* came along just in time. I am sick unto death of my own prayers, and suspect God too is tired of rolling his eyes at my words. Why am I so careful in my writing and so careless in my prayers? Bill and Isbell are renewing not only my prayers but my heart."

Leslie Leyland Fields, author of *Forgiving Our Fathers and Mothers*

"Many of us live with a severely disordered view of God. *Finding God in the Verbs* is a genuinely practical and fun help. With an inviting conversational tone, Jennie and Brent reveal how language shapes and guides our prayers and ultimately unlocks our hearts into a deeper, more intimate relationship of joy and ease with God."

Nathan Foster, Spring Arbor University, author of *Wisdom Chaser* and *The Making of an Ordinary Saint*

"*Finding God in the Verbs* ... is especially for those whose prayer life is not very meaningful anymore. It is a new way to pray. The book exercises begin with you where you are now and lead you into a new way to pray that is authentic, real and life giving."

Bob Haden, director, Haden Institute

"Brent Bill and Jennie Isbell have collaborated to create a compelling, life-changing book on prayer. They will engage you, with gracious and penetrating questions, to explore the heart of your relationship with God, while also guiding your adventure in growing that very relationship—and thus your life of prayer. This is a book for individuals wanting to deepen a life of prayer, as well being as an engaging guide to small groups considering what a 'real' life of prayer could mean for them. I plan to use this book again and again in small groups, retreats, sermons and in spiritual direction."

Stephanie Ford, author of *Kindred Souls*

"In this practical yet profound guide to prayer, two lovers of language suggest rethinking habitual ways of communicating with God. Highly recommended for all who long to articulate the silent yearnings, hidden fears, private sorrows and burning joys of the soul—and particularly for those pastors, spiritual directors and soul friends who accompany them along the path."

Paula Huston, author of *The Holy Way*

"Early in my reading of *Finding God in the Verbs,* I came to the line that said, 'Both of us find that when we pray we enter into mystery.' That's when I knew the book was true—that it was written by those who understand the power of prayer and the divine portal that it presents to our human hearts. One that, if we dare, offers entry into the Holy of Holies and conversation with the Creator. In that, there be deep magic."

River Jordan, author of *Praying for Strangers*

To my mother, Kay, who taught me why to pray.

—Jennie

To my wife, Nancy, whose life is prayer and prayer is life.

—Brent

1

A New Way to Pray

May these words of my mouth and this meditation of my heart be pleasing in your sight, LORD, my Rock and my Redeemer.

PSALM 19:14

What's that you say?" That's what a hard-of-hearing grandparent used to demand of Brent and his slang-wielding, fast-talking cousins. A few well-chosen words were what was wanted—not a bunch of idle chatter.

"What's that you say?" While God is not some elderly grandparent in the sky, we wonder if God might be longing to say that to us sometimes. That's probably because, at times, we've begun to mumble. We've forgotten to pray from our hearts. We've stopped listening for the Spirit working within us. We've lost our connection to God. We've found that we no longer draw out our own words from deep within our souls. So, we have hungered for a new way of praying—a way that reconnects us to the most important conversation of our lives.

A few summers ago, Jennie offered a workshop called Seeking and Finding God in the Verbs for a meeting of Quakers in Plainfield, Indiana. The title intrigued Brent and he signed up for it. As Jennie led the overflow workshop group, participants delightedly called out verbs and worked their way toward new nouns to use in addressing God in prayer. The room was full of energy.

We had lunch after the workshop. As we chatted and ate, Jennie mentioned that she came up with this workshop because she wanted to help people connect more authentically to God in their prayer life. Brent replied that workshop certainly worked for him.

> *I told Jennie that what I learned in her workshop that morning was going to change the way I prayed. Using what she had taught in that little more than an hour brought a fresh desire to pray deeper and more authentically. I said that I wanted to write a book with her based on her workshop. Her ideas about language and how words matter—informing both what we are saying in prayer and what we want to pray—was something people would resonate with and find really helpful.*

A few years have passed since that lunch conversation. We've had a number of chats since then—a large number! The book you have in your hands is the result of those conversations about prayer—the conversation of prime importance in our lives. This book is about a new way of praying that we want to share with you.

THE MOST IMPORTANT CONVERSATION

We both recognized the importance of prayer early in our lives. We had good teachers. Brent remembers nighttime prayers at home, grace at meals at his and neighbors' homes, prayer meetings at church, and his grandmother having other old women (probably in their sixties!) kneel in her living room for prayer. And Jennie says:

> *I learned to pray from the women in my life, particularly my mother. It was not the words for prayer that I got from her, but the heart for it. I cannot count the number of times she said to me, "Jennie, the good Lord doesn't give you anything you can't handle." That's just not the way it works—everything about her ceaseless optimism was undergirded by this belief. And, I believed her. I remember as a little girl watching her mouth shape soundless words while driving, while cleaning house, while cooking dinner. I knew this was the ongoing conversation at the center of my mother's life.*
>
> *As a girl, I strained to hear the words—my mother's to God, God's back to my mother, and God's back to me as I began my own conversation. Truthfully, I can't remember much*

of what I prayed about back then. The quality of the conversation was enough to keep me going.

We learn from hearing or reading the prayers of others. That is why this book is peppered with the prayers of our friends and colleagues. You will find them in the sidebars. They are authentic, deep prayers and we hope you will find them inspiring you to the same.

All of these experiences showed us the significance of a rich prayer life. We felt the quality of the conversation. It kept us going. For a while. And then we found ourselves slipping into patterns of oft-repeated prayers that weren't up to the task of spiritually nourishing communication with God. These were snack-bar, microwave-meal and TV-dinner equivalents of prayer instead of homegrown, home-cooked, made-in-love sort of prayers that we had been fed by in innumerable ways. Or we stopped praying at all, expecting God the all-knowing to read our minds and hearts and be satisfied.

When we sat down one afternoon over coffee to chat, we admitted to each other that we had prayer concerns. They weren't the kind that are often mentioned in worship on Sunday mornings. For Brent, it was finding himself saying the same words over and over. He did this because growing up as a non-liturgical Quaker, he relied on unstructured, informal prayers.

I was taught those were the only authentic prayers. Liturgical, written prayers, like my Catholic playmates prayed, were not truly prayer because they were the vain repetitions that Jesus preached against. The only real prayer had to spring spontaneously from the soul—a movement of the Spirit in my childhood heart.

Of course, such teaching didn't exactly square with "Now I Lay Me Down to Sleep," "God Is Great," and other prayers I'd been encouraged to memorize. Still, that thought—that true prayer has to arise unplanned from the heart—influences how I pray today.

Jennie, on the other hand, learned in college the love of praying the Psalms and prayers from ancient Christians. She loved the feeling of companionship that she sensed in repeating their words, and she experienced gratitude for their transparency in their struggles. That transparency was apparent in their words of pleading and their words of celebration. However, she also found that relying too much on another's prayers of intimacy with God inhibited the ripening of her own relationship with the Holy One.

At another meeting, while our coffee cooled and the shared scone disappeared, we admitted that, spontaneously or via a prayer book, we often heard the same words coming out of our mouths time and again. We found ourselves longing for something more;

something richer. We imagined God bored with our seemingly desultory, superficial stanzas. We knew we were.

We don't think we're the only Christians who feel this way. People are hungry to pray authentically. Just look at the overwhelming response to Anne Lamott's bestselling book *Help, Thanks, Wow: The Three Essential Prayers.* These are genuine, from-the-heart prayers. Judging by the book's sales, they resonated with readers. Perhaps that's because many of us have prayed those words. They have sprung directly from our souls and made their way out through our mouths. People of faith through the years have prayed them. As Meister Eckhart says, "If the only prayer you ever say in your entire life is thank you, it will be enough." Help, thanks and wow are essential. And they're enough if prayed with a real sense of need, gratitude and inspiration that feeds our souls and connects us with God.

> Please dear God, thank you for the amazing opportunities you have given me to answer to that of God in other people.
>
> **Elaine Emmi**

But we admit that it was easy for us to lapse into repetitious refrains, refrains that felt less than sufficient to carry us into the deep waters of the Spirit we longed to dive into. Our hearts told us that we had lapsed into easy God-speak. We weren't reaching deep into our spirits and drawing out living words of praise, confession, concern, intercession and longing. We were tired of speaking in clipped shorthand to God. We wanted to pray in such a way that we showed up with our whole selves.

The first action in changing the way we pray is to bring to light and to mind our individual habits of prayer. This book offers companionship and guidance as you begin to notice, consider, and deepen your prayer experiences. We include exercises in every chapter to bring the content to life, to *your* life. Reflection and reflectively writing your way through this book will make reading it a richer experience.

EXERCISE 1—THE USUAL PRAYER SUSPECTS

Take out your journal and a pen or pencil. Take a few moments and make a list of the prayers you use regularly. Write them out as fully as you can. We will revisit this list later.

- your daily prayers

- your special-occasion prayers

- your go-to prayers

- written prayers that you enjoy

PRACTICING PRAYERS OF INSPIRED IMPERFECTION

Part of the holy experiment we propose with prayer language involves practicing inspired and imperfect prayers.

Inspired sounds pretty good, doesn't it? Imperfect, less so. After all, doesn't Scripture urge us to "be perfect, therefore, as your heavenly Father is perfect" (Matthew 5:48)? How can we bring imperfect prayers before the perfect God?

We can't if we think our imperfection is a surprise to God. We believe that thinking our imperfections might startle God is one reason we held back from using words and images that were the truest expressions of our reaching to God—especially when our imperfections are not huge ones. As Brent says,

> *It would be easier for me to confess something big to God. Then, in the face of such holiness, a deep failing would come as no surprise. As if God is ever surprised. But it's the pettiness of my imperfections that makes it hard to pray authentically and imperfectly in some ways. Shouldn't I be a better person now after all these years of following the way of Jesus? Has God been keeping close enough tabs on me to know that I can often be hateful, mean-spirited, impatient and riddled with imperfection? In my*

head I say, "Yes, God knows," but my heart says, "Keep it hidden just in case."

As we talked about this in another coffee shop (we drank a lot of coffee while working on this book!), we decided that when we bring our whole hearts and our willingness to be changed by praying in a new way, God delights in our efforts. After all, we reasoned, we weren't the first imperfect pray-ers. "Happy is the one who seizes your infants and dashes them against the rocks" (Psalm 137:9) hardly sounds like a prayer that would please the God who is love. Nope, not even our imperfections set us apart from the great remembered prayers and pray-ers of preceding generations. What we learned from them as we looked at their prayers is that their relationship with God was so consuming, so inspiring, so fearless, that they used *their* own words. Stories of people being called to God permeate Scripture. We see this as inspiration to consider what ways God calls us to live and pray more authentically.

> God, please guide me, let faith fill my heart instead of fear.
>
> **Jana Llewellyn**

Throughout this book we're going to invite you into new ways of using *your* own words! There will be times that the language may feel awkward or out of sync with your faith life. However, we have found that being stretched beyond the familiar helped us move beyond fearing that, in the most intimate relationship of our lives, our words would be insufficient. The exercises we offer to you opened us in a fresh way to the great lover of our souls. Risking using our own words in an original approach helped us to know God (and ourselves) a bit more as we were known by God.

We continue to discover our habits of prayer even as we change them. In fact, upon closer examination, it may be that this process of discovery of our prayer habits, and of where our language and understandings rise from, *is* the key to changing them. We rarely intentionally seek to change things that fly under the radar of our self-awareness. The hunger for something deeper, more authentic, however, awakens new eyes to see ourselves with. The next exercise will help you begin to see your prayers and prayer habits from a few steps back, which will enable you to see them woven into your larger prayer life and relationship with God.

EXERCISE 2—THE SOURCE OF PRAYER

Take out your journal and a pen or pencil. Now take a moment and say a prayer aloud. Where did you go for your prayer? Did it spring spontaneously from your soul? From your memory? From a prayer book?

The source does not matter so much as does an awareness of the source. If you read the entire exercise before saying a prayer, notice what thoughts informed your prayer choice.

Write your reflections about the words you used. You might find it helpful to write the "important" words down.

Were the words

- bold?

- safe?

- edgy?

- perfect or imperfect?

- accurate reflections of how you feel and believe?

And so we begin. As we thought of an image for what we're proposing, we came up with tidying a sock drawer. It is often best to take all the socks out, match up lost pairings in sensible ways, and then re-roll and make a perfect display that is easy to access.

Of course, deep and authentic prayer isn't anything like a tidy drawer. But the metaphor, with some limits, does work. This book is a process. It's staged in chapters with guided exercises to move you through the process of inventorying and clarifying what is tucked away in your "prayer drawer" and how it got there.

Sometimes we get into a rut. We only wear the first five pairs of socks. Our favorites that are always at the front of the drawer. Other socks get shoved to the back. This can be true in prayer as well. In the next chapter, we examine our go-to prayer words and what we can learn by following the thread of them to their origin as our favorites.

2

What Lies Beneath the Words

*They replied, "Some say John the Baptist; others say Elijah;
and still others, one of the prophets."
"But what about you?" he asked. "Who do you say I am?"*

MARK 8:28-29

Who do you say I am?" That's a question we often prefer to leave to theologians. The fact is, though, that we are theologians. Yes, we mean Jennie and Brent are. But we also mean that *you* are. All of us people of faith are. We have been our entire spiritual journeys. Our theological training begins early and is pervasive. In Jennie's childhood congregation, there were many women tending to the education and care of the children. Singing was a primary means of training children to be little theologians, skilled to talk about the nature of God. Songs like "He's Got the Whole World in His Hands" and "Jesus Loves Me" formed the basis of the children's theology. They certainly set the stage for their conversations with God.

Theology is translated as God talk. Another definition of theology is "faith seeking understanding." We have found that the journey toward an authentic prayer life, in which prayer is a never-ending conversation with God, begins with what St. Anselm called "faith seeking evidence." Our faith doesn't seek such evidence to prove God's existence. Rather, we seek evidence so that we can step closer to the intimacy we desire in our relationship with God.

Jennie experienced seeking evidence—in a difficult way—when she was in high school.

I hit a wall in prayer, and in my faith life in general, when my father was hospitalized with what seemed to be a life-threatening illness. I remember having my first argument with God, a big one. I threatened to stop speaking to God because of what had happened to my dad. Perhaps this is a typical hurdle for teens grasping for a more mature faith that also addresses the new questions that come with puberty and new social expectations as they prepare for college or life after school. What strikes me now as I think back on these angry prayers I sent out to God is that I was blaming God. I wasn't bargaining for a better outcome. I was blaming God because God had let me down. God did not, as far as I could see, have the world and my father, in hand. And if they were in hand, how careless. My dad recovered and lived to be eighty-four, but this break-up with God was deeply uncomfortable for me. The worldview I had built from my mother's example and the words of teaching songs from the Sunday school ladies was insufficient and in dire need of reconstruction. But I had no idea where to begin. My basic understandings were shattered and I stood among the rubble, preparing to go to college. With my words-of-Jesus-in-red Bible in one arm and a short stack of Christian biographies in the other, I set out to learn about my tradition.

The exercises in this book largely grow out of Jennie's sense that asking better questions produces better answers. To know what worldview we carry and where it comes from begins to move us beyond the possibility of hitting a wall such as the one Jennie hit as a young woman. When considering questions about our long-held beliefs, we discover gaps or weak spots in our worldview. Eventually we end up with a stronger faith foundation.

Within the limits of a human lifetime, we grow and learn in the life of faith. The communal nature of the Christian tradition, growing out of its Jewish roots, allows ways for group and cross-generational understandings of our Creator and Sustainer. We learn from others to see God and the faith in new ways. As we direct our attention to the language of God, we come closer to lively and inspiring understandings of our glimpses of our Sustainer. One piece of evidence is the language others use to talk about

God. By examining the actions, names and adjectives attributed to God by generations of "God watchers" who have preceded us, we come to know more of the story of human interaction with the divine Mystery. Yes, God is outside of time and beyond complete human comprehension. Still, we come to know God through experience (personal and learning as a part of our faith communities). Words are a part of that experience.

Though in this book we are literally talking about parts of speech—verbs, nouns and so on—what we are really addressing are narrative and story. Narrative and story are how verbs, nouns and other parts of language come together to create a radically different way of praying.

By opening ourselves to fresh images of God through looking for evidence in our lives and the lives of our spiritual ancestors, reading Scripture, and taking hold of new words, we receive new glimpses of God. All of these invite us deeper into relationship with God.

The idea of seeking and finding God in the verbs is geared toward helping us see how God moves in the world and in our lives. God-spotting is an art, not a science. It is part of a new way of praying that takes us deeper while at the same time keeping our focus on the holy relationship between God and us.

The Prayer Before the Crucifix at San Damiano
Most High, glorious God,

enlighten the darkness of my heart

and give me true faith,

certain hope and perfect charity,

sense and knowledge, Lord,

that I may carry out

Your holy and true command.

St. Francis of Assisi (1181–1226)

THE WORDS WE CHOOSE

Scripture tells us that God knows our thoughts. This can be either comforting or scary, depending on what our thoughts are! As we talked about the implications of this, we had to consider the logical conclusion. If God knows our thoughts as they form, then God knows our words as we choose them too. If that's true, then are words relatively unimportant in the holy relationship? Who needs words if God, in effect, has a pre-show, pre-edit viewing of our prayers? And who needs a book on words and prayer? We could quit talking and writing (and drinking so much coffee).

But words do matter. At least to us.

We knew they mattered to us because as we sat and chatted we saw how we formed our emotions and thoughts into words that communicated our ideas with each other. Our words mattered to us, individually and as two people having a conversation. As we discussed, argued and agreed about prayer, we concluded that forming our mind's and heart's intentions into words to communicate with God is one of the most important processes in our spiritual lives. After all, if the act of putting words to thought so that the thoughts could be expressed mattered that much in a coffee shop conversation, how much more important was doing that in prayer? Forming words of prayer rallies all that we are and all that we hope to be into clear intention. When we write or speak our prayers, we release these intentions like an arrow from a bow, with the single-focused aim of being seen and heard as we truly are.

Yes, if we approach God with honesty and transparency, we acknowledge that God already knows our hearts, souls, dreams, failings, aspirations, minds and intentions. But by putting words to our prayers, we acknowledge to ourselves what *we* know of hope, fear and challenge. Our words help us reach toward God with the truth of who we are and what we long for. They also encourage, enhance and confirm our willingness to be changed—when we use authentic, truthful words, that is. We admitted to each other that there were times we weren't always willing to be changed. Change is not always comfortable or easy. Change is, as spiritual writer Emilie Griffin says, "very dangerous business."

For all the benefits it offers of growing closer to God, it carries with it one great element of risk: the possibility of change. In prayer we open ourselves to the chance that God will do something with us that we had not intended. We yield to possibilities of intense perception, of seeing through human masks and the density of "things" to the very center of reality. This possibility is exciting, but at the same time there is a fluttering in the stomach that goes with any dangerous adventure.

Don't we know for a fact that people who begin by "just praying"—with no particular aim in mind—wind up trudging off to missionary lands, entering monasteries, taking part in demonstrations, dedicating themselves to the poor and sick? To avoid this, sometimes we excuse ourselves from prayer by doing good works on a carefully controlled schedule.

That's why learning and listening to the language we use in prayer is vital. The words we use reveal what we believe about God, ourselves and the divine-human relationship. Finding God in the verbs leads us to deeper insight into ourselves and our faith. It also moves us toward the God who knows us and wishes to be known by us. That's why we believe that our words are important to God too. The next exercise will help you to begin to create a catalog of your prayer words. This exercise is about taking a few steps back from your prayer habits in order to see the threads that are woven into the bigger picture.

EXERCISE 3—PRAYER WORDS

Take out your journal and a pen or pencil. Make a list of the words you use when you pray.

- What names for God do you use?

- What verbs do you rely on in each of the different kinds of prayer you make—intercessory prayers ("please"), praise prayers ("wow") and gratitude prayers ("thanks")?

- What adjectives do you use?

THE LENSES

We both have imperfect vision, as many people do. If you've been for an eye exam, you are familiar with the soundtrack "Which is better, one or two? Two or three? Three or one?" This opportunity to consider which lens is a better fit is an important aspect of self-care. It helps us check the accuracy of what we *think* we see.

While not all of us wear glasses or contact lenses, we all wear unique lenses through which we see friends, family, faith, the world and God. Sometimes we've been wearing these lenses so long that we forget that we have them on. That's why we may not see how they affect our prayers. Until, that is, we take them off or have them checked.

One of the main lenses we wear is *embedded theology.* While you may not be familiar with it, you have it. We all do. Embedded theology is beliefs about God (theo-ology = God talk) that become so much a part of us that they are "embedded," often unconsciously. Because of that it is often hard for us to see that some of what we believe may not be essential. In fact, some of what we believe may be cultural—in the same way that much of what we believe about Christmas (three wise men, for example) comes from holiday songs, not Scripture.

So how did we come to believe many of the things we consider bedrock? *We chose them.* Brent's continual references to the Bible come largely from the primacy his Evangelical Friends church placed on Scripture. His belief that peace-making means not participating in war comes from the Bible, his pacifist Quaker roots and his own coming of age during the Vietnam War when he had to deal with that issue head-on. Jennie's deep sense of the importance of extending hospitality and help comes from her father. He lived from this orientation because his mother was raised in a Baptist orphanage and taught these values at home. Jennie gets her conviction that Jesus' teaching stories are important from growing up with a Bible that emphasized his words in red ink.

Regardless of where these beliefs came from, we chose them because they "fit" for us. Often they began to fit well before we were thinking critically. Maybe even when we were children. They became embedded. The is true for all of us.

Since this embedded theology is one of the main lenses through which we see God (and the world), we need to have our spiritual eyes checked occasionally. When we examine our spiritual lenses, we have the chance to change our prescription to one that uses ideas and practices that bring us closer to God. Then we have clear, not blurry, spiritual vision. Changing our lenses may mean that we have to unchoose some things we've considered "essential" since childhood.

Lens examination happens for a variety of reasons. It might be a routine exam, like Brent has every year. Or some drastic vision impairment may drive us to have our lenses checked. This is what happened, physically, to Brent when he suddenly had difficulty seeing the slides in a presentation he attended years ago. Following the class, he had a vision exam and got new glasses. Days later, he was using a home vision chart as part of a job application packet and couldn't read the chart. Three days later he was diagnosed with diabetes. This diagnosis came only as a result of his rapid vision loss, which turns out to be one of the symptoms of a much larger problem that required more than new lenses.

When such a call for change or an unsettling event happens (physically or spiritually), what we have always thought of as undisputable suddenly leaves us questioning. When a loved one dies, we may ponder heaven. When something terrible happens to someone apparently good, we might question mercy. When what we have in our catalog of beliefs does not seem to meet our needs in the face of a current situation, we might begin examining those beliefs more closely. This is called *deliberative theology.* Deliberate theology is theology that is intentional and considered before being adopted. Only after that process is it integrated as a lens through which we see and reflect on the events of our lives.

Examinations and reshapings happen at different times for different people. For some of us, spiritual examinations happen many times across our lifetime! It's part of our pursuing faithfulness. Others take longer between examinations. Still others avoid examinations all together.

One reason for long periods or delays may be that such examinations aren't always comfortable. After all, it puts us and our lenses under the divine microscope. There our lenses are polished, edges smoothed and our relationship with God reshaped. This is good—but not always comfortable since our lenses (especially the embedded theology one) don't pop out as easily as contact lenses.

We need to be aware of our lenses if we want to grow deep in prayer and our relationship with God. Our lenses inform both how we see God and the words we form in prayer. The following exercise offers a bit of a "vision test." It will help you to begin to see your lenses in action. There are no wrong answers on this test. Enjoy getting in touch with your beliefs and the words you would use to describe them.

EXERCISE 4—MY BELIEF LENSES

Take out your journal and a pen or pencil. Spend a few minutes completing the following statement (in as few or many words as you want), inserting each of the following words into the blank. "What I believe about _____ is":

- God

- the Bible

- heaven

Now look at your statements. Following each one, list your sources for these beliefs (for example, Sunday school, personal Bible reading, church doctrine and so on).

Reflect on these statements of belief as your lenses. Notice which beliefs are the result of deliberation and which ones are embedded. There may be some that are both. We will revisit lenses and the beliefs they indicate soon.

FURTHER LENS CHECKS

We now offer you some additional, brief lens checks. Like actual vision checks, there's no one or expected right answer. The only correct answer is one that is honest and revealing and helps you become aware of the lenses you're wearing.

Check one. Jesus referred to God as a mother hen. In Luke 13:34, Jesus is speaking to some Pharisees when he says, "How often I have longed to gather your children together, as a hen gathers her chicks under her wings." How does this mother hen image strike you? Is it funny? uncomfortable? comforting?

Check two. The verb in this passage shows God's action of *gathering* chicks under wing. The compound noun that goes with this is *mother hen.* So what might a prayer to God as Mother Hen sound like? What needs and longings might it express? Here's what Jennie came up with:

> O Great Mother Hen,
> How I long to feel your wings surround me.
> How I miss the comfort of days in the egg,
> before being forced to grow and stretch my
> unformed wings!
> Mother Hen, show me how. I know nothing.
> Come and sit upon me, giving shelter and warmth
> as you did when I was helpless in egg.

Reread this prayer. How does it affect you? Do you feel kinship with the prayer's longing? Do you feel invited into a fresh image of God that is incomplete but compelling? Do you find it unsettling? Your reactions are dependent greatly on the lenses you wear.

Remember, "mother hen" is a biblical metaphor. The reason we used this particular metaphor from Scripture is that it gives us an entry point into our own feelings. Regardless of what they are.

Was your reaction positive? When we enter into an image with our longing to be intimate with God's help paramount, we find authentic words. We find words that show our intention and need and that spring from our souls. This image speaks to Jennie's heart. It opens up a way for her to express her soul's deepest longing with genuine, heartfelt, mind-enlarging words.

> To the Ground of All Being, the source of life and love, grant us today a glimpse into the mystery of life itself and expand our hearts to find better ways of loving those we live with, share our journey with, and may have an impact upon. Forgive us, and enable us to forgive others. Bring peace to the world. Come, Lord Jesus, quickly come. Amen.
>
> **Tom Rugh**

Was your response negative? When we encounter an image that discomforts us, we can look and see why it does. There was a time that Jennie's prayer would have set Brent's spiritual teeth on edge. It went against his understanding of God culturally and religiously, based on his embedded theology that only masculine words should be used to refer to God.

It doesn't matter what our reaction is. What matters is our examination of it. That's because when we examine our reaction, we're doing a lens check. We begin to think about whether our lenses are helping us see aright—or whether some adjustment might be needed.

As we move through this book, we'll be looking at language (including metaphor) and prayer. We want you to be prepared to be stretched and challenged—as we were when we began praying this way.

THREE KEY QUESTIONS

Once we learn that we have lenses and that our prayer words express the reality of those lenses, we move more deeply into a mature faith. Early on as we worked on this book, Jennie taught Brent three questions that moved him deeper in prayer.

- What do the words I pray imply about God's nature?

- What do the words I pray imply about human nature or humanity?

- What do the words I pray imply about the relationship between God and me as a human being?

Our answers to these questions have come to be at the center of our prayer language. In fact, they have become the center of our lives. They help us think about how we live and move and have our being as people of faith.

Pick up your journal. Go to "Exercise 3—Prayer Words." That's the exercise where you listed the names for God, the verbs and adjectives you use most when you pray. Look at your words through the lens of the three questions.

- What do the words I pray say about God's nature? "God is..."

- What do the words I pray say about human nature or humanity? "Humans are..."

- What do the words I pray say about the relationship between God and me as a human being? "The relationship between God and humanity is..."

You might be surprised what your pondering reveals. Did you realize you thought these things about God? About the human condition? Do they reflect some things that make you uncomfortable? Do they affirm what you believe?

We must enter the conversation with God by bringing our full selves if we wish to have a true life of prayer. We propose that one doorway to an authentic prayer life is through language. The conversation of prayer, after all, is communication through words, spoken or unspoken. By praying, we clarify and express our intention with a level of focus that does not often grace the rest of our daily life.

Hold these three questions about God and humanity close. Use them to understand and deepen your prayer words. Especially keep them in mind as we move together through this book. Use them to guide you into the deep waters of soulful prayer.

DANCING WITH GOD IN PRAYER

As we've said, our conversation was about going deeper in prayer. We longed for a closeness to God. A fresh way of praying—with words that were deep and genuine with our experience and aspirations—seemed to be the means by which our longing could become reality. The following piece by St. Augustine shows us a glimpse into the inescapable intimacy of our connection with God by describing it as a dance.

> I praise the dance, for it frees people
> from the heaviness of matter and binds the
> isolated to community.
> I praise the dance, which demands everything:
> health and a clear spirit and a buoyant soul.

> Dance is a transformation of space, of time, of people,
> who are in constant danger of becoming all brain, will, or feeling.
> Dancing demands a whole person,
> one who is firmly anchored in the center of his life,
> who is not obsessed by lust for people and things
> and the demon of isolation in his own ego.
> Dancing demands a freed person,
> one who vibrates with the equipoise of all his powers.
> I praise the dance.
> O man, learn to dance,
> or else the angels in heaven will not know what to do with you.

When we changed Augustine's "dance" to "prayer," we saw the power and glory of the holy conversation to which we were invited. Read Augustine's words aloud. Substitute "prayer" for "dance." In such prayer, we claim our identity as people of the incarnation. Through such prayer, we choose and use words that speak the truth of our connection with God.

We invite you to join with us in learning to dance in prayer with God. Join us in the unending, inescapable conversation between Creator and created! When we enter this conversation, we find ourselves transformed. We leave our old lenses behind and find ourselves freely stepping deeper into the conversation with God.

3

God in Action

FINDING OUR VERBS

In the beginning God created the heavens and the earth.

GENESIS 1:1

*The man and his wife heard the sound of the LORD God
as he was walking in the garden
in the cool of the day.*

GENESIS 3:8

The LORD God made garments of skin for Adam and his wife and clothed them.

GENESIS 3:21

This is, without a doubt, one of my favorite items ... uh ... 'My Dinner with Andre' action figures."

This is a snippet from Christopher Guest's *Waiting for Guffman,* a quirky comedy that is one of Brent's favorite films.

The whole premise (a group of small-town actors putting on a play in which the director uses his very dubious connections to New York theater to invite producer Max Guffman to town in the belief that Guffman will take the play [and them!] to Broadway), and what ensues, is hilarious and slightly sad. The end is especially poignant, as Corky St. Clair (Guest) talks about his new shop that sells theater memorabilia. His pride in having action figures from a movie that has no action is ironic—though he doesn't get the irony.

One night while watching that scene I thought of that in the context of prayer. It's just how some of my prayers are. I claim to believe that God is a God of action who is involved in the affairs of humankind, but I often pray as if I believe God is passive. At least based on the verbs I use.

God as an inaction figure.

We know from our experience and from Scripture (like the ones cited at the beginning of this chapter) that God is active. How then do we begin to move our prayer words for God out of passivity into activity? How do we go from a God whom we pray *at* to a God who is active in our lives? The next exercise will help you notice whether your prayers paint God as mostly active or mostly passive.

EXERCISE 5—CURRENT VERBS

Take out your journal and a pen or pencil. Take a few moments and look over your previous journal exercises. What verbs about God appear in them? What are you asking God to do, or acknowledging that God has done? List them in your journal.

Then think about other verbs you use when you pray. These would be verbs that relate to you—what you've done, what you want God to help you do and so on. Write them down as well.

Next look over the list. Are your verbs active (God does something—"Bless us, O Lord") or passive (God is the recipient of the action—"O Lord, we bless your holy name")?

Then reflect on the following variations of the three questions introduced in chapter one:

• What does my use of primarily passive or active verbs in prayer say about God's nature?

• What does my use of primarily passive or active verbs in prayer say about human nature or humanity?

• What does my use of primarily passive or active verbs in prayer say about the relationship between God and me as a human being?

Notice if you converse with God in your prayers as though you expect action. And notice, too, what thoughts, judgments and feelings come up as you consider this particular characteristic of your lens.

WHERE THE VERBS COME FROM

Our verbs, like all of the language we use, come from a variety of sources. Childhood and culture are two of them. Brent, for example, says, "It's time to red up the table after dinner." That's an idiom for clearing the dishes and tidying up. It comes both from his culture (a parent with a Scottish heritage) and childhood (where it was a common phrase, as in "Brent, red up the dishes").

That's why, when we pray, it's natural for us to use verbs from childhood and culture. We also add verbs from other sources. Our church, Scripture, prayers of the saints and our experiences are just a few of them. We'll look at some of these sources so that we better understand where the verbs we use now came from. As we do that, we'll discover some action verbs that we can add to our prayer vocabulary. Verbs that take us deeper into relationship with God.

Childhood. As a young child, Jennie had a vision of God as a man, sitting on a throne, with a golf bag full of lightning bolts.

> *He was like a nonjovial Santa Claus, and he preferred men, because they were more like him, and of course better in every way. My childhood faith community was very devoted to Jesus and*

the pastor and elders often emphasized that Jesus was the only child of God—a beloved Son. I was confused when I learned the Lord's Prayer, which begins, of course, with "Our Father." I could not understand how I could claim God as my parent, if Jesus was God's only child. It was worse that Jesus was a son, and the elders of my church constantly emphasized the superiority of men over women in the eyes of God. And because I grew up in a family in which the eldest son died, as a child I struggled with childish logic and a literal mind. I believed that daughters could never replace sons, especially ones who had died. Yet, Jesus himself had gifted this prayer to all of us.

We hope Jennie's confession makes you smile. We also hope you caught the beginning of her undoing: Jesus taught the Lord's Prayer or "Our Father" to be a prayer of *inclusion* to all who said it. This is Jennie's first remembered faith paradox. It fueled theological difficulties that led to a period of spiritual dryness and abstention from prayer in her teen years. It simply didn't make sense to say that Jesus, as the *only* child of God, would teach her to pray using inclusive, sibling language—"Our Father. Give us. Lead us."

As children in church, we thrilled to Jesus' respect and love for children. We sang with happy hearts:

Jesus loves the little children
All the children of the world
Red, brown, yellow, black or white

> They're all precious in his sight
> Jesus loves the little children of the world

The stories we learned and songs we sang as children helped us understand that our relationship to God is intimate, like a child to her parent. They remind us today of the unguarded, open and loving nature of a child who has not yet taken on the burdens of adulthood and rationality, and that God is loving. They also remind us that, while Jesus' praises a childlike nature, he doesn't encourage immaturity and childishness. As Aldous Huxley writes:

> A childlike adult is not one whose development is arrested; on the contrary, he is an adult who has given himself a chance of continuing to develop long after most people have muffled themselves into a cocoon of middle age habit and convention.

That is why, in the process of claiming a richer prayer language for prayer, we examine the images of God we received as children. We do so to learn what we believe about God, human nature and our relationship with God. As we have more experiences of life and difficulty, it is important to our faithfulness that our beliefs "work" when put to the test of making sense of our lived experiences.

Scripture. *Bible Picture ABC Book* is one of the oldest books sitting on Brent's shelves.

I've had it for what seems my whole life. It's pretty beat up (it went through me and my three sisters). But it's a treasure. Arranged in alphabetical order is an assortment of Bible stories that kids would relate to. The left page had a color lithograph illustration of the story, and the right-hand side had a short story, with a reference to the actual Scripture the story referred to and some Bible vocabulary words. My favorite was S is for Samuel. The story was titled "The Boy Who Heard God's Voice." It opened to me the possibility that I might hear God's voice too. Even as a kid—even if I didn't look as holy as the picture of Samuel on the facing page.

That book—and its source, the Bible—gave me a lot of active verbs for God. God talked, God walked, God created, God helped.

There wasn't anything God didn't do!

Fortunately, that cherished book was not the extent or end of Brent's learning from the Bible. He and Jennie continue to explore the Bible for action verbs related to God and God's action and interaction with humankind. For example, in the story of Cain and Abel, we see God

- accepting
- rejecting

- asking questions

- punishing

- protecting

That's a lot of verbs in just one story! But the beginning of Genesis is long ago and far away. It's at the start of the Bible. What do the parts of the Bible a bit closer to our time—the New Testament—say about God?

Well, in Luke 18, we see Jesus teaching a parable about a Pharisee who thanks God that he is not like a list of sinners he names. Last on his list is a tax collector. This tax collector happens to be present in the temple—also praying. The tax collector's prayer, in contrast to the Pharisee's, is simple. He beats his chest and says, "God, have mercy on me, a sinner!" (Luke 18:13). In the story we learn that God

- lowers the prideful

- raises the humble

- hears our prayers

- knows our hearts

- bestows mercy

Scripture is shot through with active verbs for God. We, though, often forget to look for them. Instead, we mostly look for the "bigger" spiritual truths behind the stories. The next time you read the Bible, take some time picking out the verbs describing God's activity. You might even pull out your journal, record them and then compose prayers based on them. How would using newfound verbs change your prayers and the way you pray?

> Holy God,
>
> Holy Strong,
>
> Holy Immortal,
>
> have mercy on us.
>
> **The Trisagion**

SAINTS: ANCIENT AND MODERN

During one of our coffee conversations, we talked about how it's not only Scripture that taught us prayer verbs; various prayer practitioners have influenced us as well. The church fathers and mothers and generations of Christian monastics and mystics up to the present presented us with verbs (and other parts of language, obviously) illuminating their encounters with God. Both of us look to them for insight and assistance with our own searches for language and connection with the Holy.

Ignatius of Loyola, who grew from a noble birth and knighthood into being a priest and hermit, founded the Jesuit order of Roman Catholic priests. In one of his prayers he pleads:

Dearest Lord, teach me to be generous;
Teach me to serve thee as thou deserves;
To give and not to count the cost,
To fight and not to seek for rest,
To labor and not to seek reward
Save that of knowing that I do thy will.

While he doesn't say straight out that God is a teacher, his words imply that God is just that. As we look carefully at his prayer, we also see that Ignatius believed that

• God has a will

• God's will can be known

• God's will can be fulfilled by humans when God teaches them what that will is

Teresa of Ávila was a Carmelite nun. Today she is best known as the author of *The Interior Castle,* a spiritual guide for encountering God through prayer and service. In one prayer, she writes:

Govern everything by your wisdom, O Lord, so that my soul may always be serving you in the way you will and not as I choose. Let me die to myself so that I may serve you. Let me live to you who are life itself. Amen.

Like Ignatius, Teresa refers to God's will. Her words imply that God

• governs

- gives life

- desires (us to serve)

Both of these Christian ancestors prayed with their lenses on. By considering their prayers, we can begin to see the beliefs that made up their lenses, and we can examine them to see if they might be good lenses for us—or if they don't work at all.

In addition to appreciating the prayers of older Christians, we both look to "newer" pray-ers, as well. We want to learn from people who are closer to the shared cultural values and challenges of our lives. Some that we find especially helpful are those that are unedited for theological soundness by any body of oversight or translating editors. These more contemporary Christians are able to share with us the varied and authentic stories of their holy conversations without the heavy editing oversight of a church council.

Howard Thurman, an African American civil rights leader, Baptist pastor and theologian in the second half of the twentieth century, wrote the prayer "Through the Coming Year."

> Grant that I may pass through the coming year with a faithful heart. There will be much to test me and make weak my strength before the year ends. In my confusion I shall often say the word that is not true and do the things of which I am ashamed.

The prayer goes on with startling self-awareness of possible failings Thurman anticipates of himself. He writes, "In seeking the light, I shall again and again find myself walking in the darkness. I shall mistake my light for Your Light."

Like Ignatius and Teresa (and David, Paul, Jesus and others), Thurman's prayer asks God to grant him a faithful heart. Maybe we can learn something about what our own intentions for prayer should be from this trend! One of the verbs implied is *gives.* God gives mercy and light, for instance.

Sometimes we look at verbs in the prayers to learn about ourselves. Henri Nouwen, a Dutch-born, Roman Catholic priest who wrote extensively on the spiritual life, offered this particularly potent prayer:

> Dear God, I am so afraid to open my clenched fists! Who will I be when I have nothing left to hold on to? Who will I be when I stand before you with empty hands?

Brent says:

> *This is a prayer I resonate with because I am often fearful and cling to things tightly. I like to be in control—even in my relationship with God. It scares me to be too vulnerable or disclosing about what's really going on inside me. Nouwen's prayer reassures me that I'm not the only one who has ever felt this way. And so it gives me the positive action verbs of opening and releasing*

and helps me discard the negative verbs of clinging and fearing.

In using a metaphor of a clenched fist to describe himself, Nouwen helps us see God as the One Who Can Help Us to Unclench. Many of us can resonate with this need to unclench. We clench our spiritual fists because we like to be in control. Even of our relationship with God. Nouwen's prayer clarifies that this tendency to fear vulnerability is part of the human condition. None of us are alone in this fear; we share it with one another. God, help us unclench. If, of course, we really want to.

The exercise that follows invites you to consider where you learned about particular actions of God. Indeed, as the old cliché puts it, "actions speak louder than words." So let's look at what actions we attribute to God.

EXERCISE 6—MY VERB SOURCES

Take out your journal and a pen or pencil. Spend a few moments looking over the previous journal exercise where you listed your verbs relating to God. Relist them here and, following each one, indicate its source. Is it from childhood? Scripture? Prayers of others? You can list more than one source for each verb.

Now, as you look over them,

- Which ones fit your beliefs and feelings today?

- Which ones might you want to consider discarding even though they're familiar or comfortable?

As you think of your favorite childhood spiritual experiences (in an organized religious setting or not), Scripture passages or saintly prayers, which of those contain verbs that might

- stretch you?

- help you pray more authentically?

- feel as though they could be your own?

- feel foreign?

GRACE-SPOTTING

"You will say, 'Christ saith this, and the apostles say this;' but what canst thou say?" That's what George Fox, the person who was the catalyst for the beginning of the Religious Society of Friends (Quakers), once asked a potential follower. It's one of our favorite Quaker quotes. As Brent says:

> *It sums up the heart of Quaker experience—that God invites us into direct relationship and experience. And then we are to put it in our words. It reminds us that while the words of the saints and mystics are beautiful and touch on the commonality of the human experience, they are*

not our words. What can we say that is true to our experience of God?

While our spiritual ancestors were interactive in their prayers, they are not our prayers. Their prayers were theirs. Their words were theirs. We need to grow our vocabulary to match our vision and experience of God. Prayer is *our* conversation with God. To rephrase Fox, "What canst thou pray?"

One way to grow our verbs is by looking for evidence of God around us—grace-spotting. Brent often does this with his camera—looking through the viewfinder for evidence of God as he walks and is gifted with pictures. As he does this, he makes lists of verbs that could be attributed to God. Walking in the woods or prairie, it's easy for him to see that God is active in creation. As the great gardener (beginning with creation, the garden in Eden, and up through today), God

- plants seeds

- rains upon

- warms

- causes seasons

- feeds the creatures

   These are all words that speak to me because they reflect my own experiences as a steward of creation. I've planted acres of tall-grass prairie with warm-season grass and wildflower seeds. I've carried water to newly planted saplings (we've planted more than twenty thousand!). I watch the seasons and witness their impact on "my garden." The trees, grasses, bushes all were planted to provide shelter and food for wildlife. Birds, rabbits, deer and more feast on a multiplicity of berry bushes, nut trees, pawpaw trees, wild cherries, and prairie pollens and seeds.

Though as a long-time city boy this is all relatively new to me, I am coming to love and care for creation in a new way. And in that love and care I am reminded, as I pray, of two important "God-verbs"—"love" and "care."

Jennie, as part of her grace-spotting, prays, "Lord, give me eyes to see." In this simple one-line prayer, she confesses that she knows that there is something to see.

I see evidence of God's presence or God's guidance perceivable by my human eyes if only they can be steadied and opened to see. It is easy to engage this mindset when I am on retreat or having a time of spiritual reflection. In the throes of life, traffic, work stress and family obligations, though, it can be challenging for me to see, or even desire to look for, God's presence in the situation.

You may do your grace-spotting by seeing God through the actions or words of other people. If that is the case, your list of God-verbs might include

- helps

- inspires

- chastises

- teaches

- causes to laugh

Because we can't always muster the focus to see the Holy (or even the desire to cultivate our awareness of God's presence), we both find it helpful to have a systematic reflective time of spiritual practice. That's why Brent carries a camera. It's why Jennie keeps a journal and writes poetry. You might want to think of a practice that will help you be more intentional in your grace-spotting. You might even want to carry your journal with you so can jot down your God-verbs. The next exercise is about reflecting on the past to do some retroactive grace-spotting.

EXERCISE 7—WHERE I HAVE PERCEIVED GOD

Take out your journal and a pen or pencil. Think about a time when you have been absolutely certain of God's presence. Recall it with as much detail as you can. Sit with your eyes closed and re-enter that experience.

As you do, turn your awareness toward the evidence that assured you that God was present.

Write the story in your journal with as much detail as you can. Emphasize God as a character in the story. You might include phrases such as

- "God opened that opportunity for me at work."

- "I felt God's presence as I walked with the question in my heart."

- "When the wind blew, I knew God was near."

Whether the appearance of God comes because you give God credit for things you actually witnessed or whether God's presence is clear to you because you "felt it" (either physically or spiritually), note your perceptions.

Highlight the action parts of your story that include God or awareness of God. Notice if there are places where you notice God's action in your life that you overlooked in real time.

ZOOMING OUT TO CHECK THE BIG PICTURE

For a moment, let's revisit those three theological questions we introduced in the first chapter. They're worded a bit differently here, but that's one of the things that makes them so useful—they are easily adapted to the task at hand.

- What does _____ say/imply about God?

- What does _____ say/imply about human nature or humanity?

- What does _____ say/imply about the relationship between God and human nature/humanity?

We're especially going to focus on question one. You've put together a number of lists and recorded lots of thoughts in your journal since you started the book. Take a few minutes to scan them all now. Can you form some summary statements about what you've written says/implies about God? It might be some thing like, "God is loving and not a punisher." Or, "God has standards and rules set for humans and spends a lot of effort reminding us to straighten up and fly right."

After you have a sentence that summarizes your belief about God, put it into the blank of the three questions. In our example, "What does the idea that God is loving and not a punisher say about God?" Or, "What does the idea that God has standards and rules and spends effort reminding us to straighten up and fly right imply about God?" You might conclude for either (or both) of our examples that God is loving and has intentions and desires for us. Both examples offer things to unpack about our deeply held understanding of the divine-human relationship.

Take some time to think up some summary statements. Let them come from your heart, soul and experience. Don't use our examples! Then relax and spend some time reflecting on your summary sense of God's character and way of being in the world. What verbs pop up in your pondering? Prayerfully consider your thoughts on God, humanity and the holy relationship.

EXERCISE 8—MY VERBS FOR TODAY

Take out your journal and pen and write as many verbs as you can that could be attributed to God. Include ones that connect with the list of ways you perceive God.

Just to be thorough, on another journal page write a list of verbs that you feel should *never* be appropriately attributed to God. This will help you identify the things that are simply beyond your image of God. Aim for at least half as many verbs on this list as you have on the list of verbs that you would attribute to God.

Take a moment to read over your two lists:

- the verbs you attribute to God

- the verbs you consider out of the bounds of the character and behavior of God

What do your verbs tell you

- about your understanding of God's character?

- about whether you see God as active or passive?

- about whether God has a basic attitude or stance?

Finally, take one of your verbs for God and compose a simple prayer based on it. For example, you might choose "create." If so, you might compose something similar to the psalmist—"Create in me a pure heart, O God" (Psalm 51:10). Or you might paraphrase Nouwen and write, "Dear God, I am so afraid. Help me open my clenched fists in offering to you." It doesn't matter what you pray. What matters is that the verb reflects the truths of your soul and your understanding of God.

> What's your verb?
> What's your prayer?
> May it be answered. Amen.

***

Word search puzzles are Brent's dad's favorite form of evening entertainment. He sits for hours looking for words hidden in the jumble of letters. He loves the sense of discovery that comes from picking out and circling the words that are hidden in plain sight. He circles them with great delight and doesn't quit until he's found them all.

That's what we're doing as we move through this book. We're offering word search puzzles for you—ones that we've used. Encircling us are new prayer words hidden in plain sight. We hope you delight in finding yours.

Next stop: nouns.

4

Images of an Active-Tense God

NOUNS THAT FIT THE VERBS

*He will be called Wonderful Counselor,
Mighty God, Everlasting Father,
Prince of Peace.*

ISAIAH 9:6

Brent has a name that some people have trouble with.

I don't understand why people frequently call me Bill Brent. People new to me do it all the time. When I correct them by saying, "My name is Brent Bill. Bill is my last name," they often reply with things like "Are you sure?" (Yes, I'm sure!) or "How'd you get a last name like that?" (Umm, my parents gave it to me) or "How odd." That last one often throws me. I've never found "Bill" odd as a last name. Unusual, perhaps, but not odd. No more odd than some of my friends' last names are to me. But I still don't confuse their last names to the first.

I'm probably too sensitive, but my name is important to me. My name has been my identifier, my badge, part of my identity as a boy, teen, young adult and man throughout my life. I would not be the person I am without it.

"What's in a name?" asks Juliet naively. As Shakespeare's *Romeo and Juliet* unfolds, we learn that everything is in a name—especially a person's name. That is true for us. It's true for our prayer vocabulary too. It's particularly true for our names for God. We all have various names we use for God. Like our verbs, they come from a variety of sources—childhood, Scripture, prayers of the saints, church doctrine and culture, and our experiences.

All of these sources influence us. They are the reason that some people feel it important to speak only of God as "God" or "Father" or "Jesus." Or that others lift prayers to the Holy Spirit. That's why in the same way that we searched for verbs that reflect the way we see God working in the world in the last chapter, we are now going to look at nouns that go with those verbs.

One of the joys that we find in grace-spotting is coming up with names that reflect what we've discovered or been reminded of about God as we're doing it. We look for images that illustrate and illuminate the character of God and the dynamics of the divine-human relationship. This next exercise is intended to walk you through creating an inventory of names for God used in prayer. We will build on this list in future exercises.

EXERCISE 9—MY NAMES FOR GOD

Take out your journal and pen. Draw a line down the middle of the page. In the left-hand column, write as many of your names for God (the ones you use in prayer and conversations about God) as you can for the next three minutes. Then move to the right-hand column and write as many of the names for God that you have heard others use, have read in Scripture and spiritual books or have heard in media (songs or videos) but have never used yourself.

Take a moment to notice which names for God come easily to you. Which are ones you encounter from other sources that don't seem to fit? If you have any strong feelings about words in either list, write a few sentences about those words.

Keep this list and date it. As you work through this book, you may decide to add to it or move words from one column to the other. Now, let's continue the work of understanding what our salutations for God have to do with authenticity in prayer.

> God who in every land and every age
>
> Has with divine compassion and divine desire
>
> Sought to reveal yourself unto us:

You who have truly shown yourself to all

Who truly have sought you

We ask that you reveal yourself to us today.

Unto us, O Loving Parent, without whom the past

has no meaning

The future has no existence

Reveal yourself in our present. Amen.

Adapted from a prayer by John S. Hoyland (1887–1958)

FROM IMAGE TO IMAGINATION AND BACK AGAIN

Because prayer is the most important conversation of our lives, how we begin our prayers is important. Many of us, when we pray, tend to start with a salutation. Brent, for instance, often begins his prayers with "O God Who Loves Us More Than We Know." Jennie prays "Loving God" when praying aloud or "Dear One" when writing in her prayer journal. We do this because we want to launch into a vital conversation. We don't want to use a lifeless, inauthentic tone or distant, rote, inherited images that keep us at an impersonal distance from the Holy. We don't want to have a reserved, cold conversation beginning with a salutation that mirrors those things. For example, Brent had a friend who, when his mother remarried, was instructed to call his new stepfather "Governor." Wow, did that set the tone for their conversations. Jennie's father was a high school gym teacher. He was called "Coach" by many, even after he had been retired for twenty-five years and his former students became grandparents. The names and titles we give one another speak volumes about the basic, enduring structures of relationship.

Since many of our names for God come from Scripture, let's start there. One of the most famous nouns describing God is *shepherd.* We encounter this image most famously, of course, in Psalm 23 (NRSV).

> The LORD is my shepherd, I shall not want.
> He makes me lie down in green pastures;
> he leads me beside still waters;
> he restores my soul.
> He leads me in right paths
> for his name's sake.
> Even though I walk through the darkest valley,
> I fear no evil;
> for you are with me;
> your rod and your staff—
> they comfort me.
> You prepare a table before me
> in the presence of my enemies;
> you anoint my head with oil;
> my cup overflows.
> Surely goodness and mercy shall follow me

all the days of my life,
and I shall dwell in the house of the Lord
my whole life long.

The psalmist describes what God makes him do: lie down and follow along as he is led by still waters. God also prepares a table and anoints the psalmist. God is active. This beloved psalm provides a good example of how we can look at the verbs and discover the nouns of God implied by Scripture.

Let's unpack the image of God as shepherd this psalm gives us. What are some of the things a shepherd does? As we brainstormed, we came up with

- herds
- feeds
- waters
- walks to better territory
- protects from attacking animals
- trains sheep to follow

What images would you add?

Look at the list of action words above to see what names or salutations for God are seeded in them. They might include

- Loving Shepherd (not surprisingly!)
- Guide

- Giver of Nourishment

- Teacher

- Source of Direction

Except for the first one, all of these salutations for the Holy carry the image of the shepherd while using fresh language based on God's actions, God's verbs. Since it comes from our minds and hearts this is language that is relevant to our spiritual needs—needs that are met by God. These names are descriptive of our relationship with God. Like the psalmist, we look to God for guidance, protection and nourishment. Our faith and tradition encourage us to depend on God for these things. Using these words that spring jointly from Scripture and from our experience of God's character bring us closer to authentic prayer.

Besides the familiar image of shepherd, this psalm also includes (via its verbs) other images. In it, God prepares a table, anoints the psalmist with oil and causes the cup to overflow. After looking at the actions of God described in it, we might begin a prayer by calling out to God as

- Divine Source

- Holy Anointer

- Filler of the Cup of My Life

You might come up with other salutations based on your reading of the psalm and your life experience. One of the exciting things about developing salutations and names for God this way is that doing so keeps us rooted in the spiritual experiences of Scripture *and* reminds us that Scripture is a powerful and relevant source of wisdom for daily life. Yes, the psalmist wrote about *his* understandings of God's presence with him. He wrote from his culture and religious life. By opening Scripture this way, we stay true to our spiritual ancestors while aligning these universal spiritual experiences with our lives and culture today. While few of us may catch a glimpse of a "real" shepherd or sheep today, we resonate with the sheep's need for care, protection, food and sustenance. Our conversation with the Holy increases in authenticity when we relate to the names and titles of reverence and praise we use in prayer without distance or unfamiliarity. That's because, on a basic level, these words make sense within the context of our real-life experiences.

Of course, God as shepherd is not the only image we can glean from the Bible. Though the psalms are alive with images, the actions of God in other scriptural books also provide us with fresh, new-to-us names. For example, the story in Genesis 17:15-19, show us that the One who gave Sarai (Sarah) a son in old age when pregnancy seemed impossible could be called the Blesser or the Opener of Wombs. If we're reading 2 Chronicles 14:11-12, we may get so caught up in the story that we fail to recognize that story gives us a new name for God. The one who protected

Asa in battle against the Cushites may be called Protector.

Scripture is filled with such opportunities for fresh, biblically grounded salutations. The next exercise guides you through a favorite passage to see what salutations are given or implied. Prepare to grow your salutation list from seeds in Scripture!

EXERCISE 10—GREETINGS AND SALUTATIONS

Take out your journal and pen. Pick a favorite passage of Scripture. If you don't have one, you might want to choose a story from the Gospels or the Psalms. These are among our favorites and are ripe with speaking about God and to God. Begin to unpack the passage by

- identifying the nouns or titles attributed to God

- making a list of the verbs that actually or could possibly go with the nouns/images

- making a list of phrases that could be used to describe God's action or character based on the Scripture passage or word

- trying out some salutations for God in prayers based on these images

Take a moment to notice how you feel with your new Scripture-inspired names for God. Notice if your role in the relationship with God is affected by a shift in the name you use. We, and our images of ourselves, can be changed by engaging Scripture in this way.

EXPANDING OUR SELF-UNDERSTANDING THROUGH PRAYER

Jennie has at times felt a disconnect when she has used "Father" solely to address God for periods in her prayer life.

> *As I mentioned earlier, the Lord's Prayer was a very important invitation for me into prayer and into seeing myself as a child of God, along with Jesus who taught the salutation "Our Father." From an early age, I was unconsciously collecting verbs that go with how a father might act, including "loves," "provides for," "disciplines," and also "withdraws from," "gets angry at" and "gives the silent treatment to." Frankly, as my relationship with my dad matured over the decades, and I became able to see and love him as another human soul on earth with far less authority than he had when I was a child, I found that using "Father" in prayer was diminishing to God because of the (completely human and natural) inconsistencies I experienced with my own father.*

If I had stayed with only "Father" as my sole salutation in prayer, I would have also stayed forever a child—a child fearing judgment and living in sadness over being a daughter instead of a son in a context where a son had died.

To force herself to use only or primarily the salutation of "Father" for God belied the truth of her experience of relating to the Holy. It resulted in less authentic conversations with God. By trying on different salutations for God, she was able to increase her compassion and love for her own father by disconnecting from a spirit-dampening loop of mental associations about fathers and our Father. Two relationships improved when she changed her prayer language: her relationship with God and with her father.

We enhance our prayer experience by entering into exploration of scriptural images. Doing so also opens up our understanding of human nature and our personal nature. Some of the salutations for God from the previous section will have greater or lesser resonance for you as you read them silently or aloud. To address God as "Loving Shepherd" implies that the pray-er is part of the herd cared for by the shepherd. To pray to God as "Teacher" or "Guide" means not only that God is in active relationship with us but also that we are teachable and can receive guidance. When God is "Anointer" or "Filler of the Cup of My Life (which is overflowing)" we are recipients of blessing and abundance. It is difficult to address God using these images if we don't feel blessed or teachable or open to guidance.

As in Jennie's story about changing her relationship with her dad through changing her prayer, however, there may be some deep, rippling effects on our own ways of being as we pray differently. Might you become more aware of feeling blessed or more open to guidance if you prayed as though it were possible?

It may be helpful to reread some of the earlier suggested salutations. See if there are some that don't fit for you. Consider these misfits. Look to see if there is something about them that paints an inconsistent picture of you or of the relationship between humanity and the Holy. If you discover a disconnect between your self-understanding and an image for God in prayer, make a note of it. Then look for the images and language that work better. Explore broadly as you look for language that will bring you to a more authentic connection with God.

In the next exercise, we'll focus on finding the names and salutations for God that grow out of the verbs you attribute to God. Notice if you are particularly drawn to verbs and images that address needs that are yours but also common to human nature.

EXERCISE 11—UNPACKING IMAGES FROM LIFE AND TRADITION

Take out your journal and review the images and verbs attributable to God that arose for you during the earlier exercises. Also write down action words for God that come from prayers from your tradition or from your personal list of ways you know God is at work in the world. Review your lists, and start a new page for the following exercise.

1. Identify the nouns or titles attributed to God and make a list of the verbs that actually or possibly would go with the noun/image.

2. Make a list of the verbs that you added to your lists.

3. Make a list of phrases that name or address the Holy based on the verbs you come up with in step 1 or 2 above. Don't rush this step. See if you can come up with at least ten.

4. Now, try out some of these salutations for God in vocal prayers based on these images.

5. After you have prayed with some of your new salutations, revisit those guiding questions from the first chapter. See if you can identify what these images or salutations imply about you personally, human nature in general, and the relationship between God and humanity.

We hope you continue to trace backward from your word lists and new experiments in prayer to begin to reflexively test what these words say or imply about God and humanity in relationship. This process of prayer is ultimately about discovering the vitality of a life lived responding to God's presence and guidance. Peeling back the layers of your understanding as you go will add clarity to this process.

PRAYING WITH NEW NAMES

Once we have salutations for God, the verbs that go with them will flow out of our daily lives and our needs in the present moment. Using new names—authentic, familiar names—changes our relationship with God. That shouldn't be surprising. We see it in our human relationships. When Brent and his wife, Nancy, first met, she jokingly called him "Mr. William."

> *"I don't know you well enough to call you Mr. Bill," she told me with a smile. As we became friends over the next years, she moved to calling me Brent. And the relationship became less formal. Later, when we dated and then married, her names for me changed. She uses different ones for different occasions—endearments for love talk, nicknames for silliness and other names for when I've done something really stupid! But we have moved way past the "Mr. William" days—and all the names she uses for me help me know*

what's on her mind, how she's feeling and what kind of action she might be looking for from me. A hug. A kiss. A job she wants me to do. Or something she wants me to stop doing!

That can be true for us as well in prayer. For example, when we address God as Shepherd, we chose a name that implies we might be looking for certain things from our relationship—for God to take us to better ground, to rest or to call us back to the herd, for example. Using Shepherd allows us to approach God with vulnerability and honesty based on our authentic needs.

Jennie put together a few prayers based on the Shepherd image, just to show how to do this.

In a time of feeling as if my needs are not being met, I might pray:

> Dear Shepherd, I cannot feel your presence. I go hungry for spiritual sustenance and thirsty for cool water. I and my life feel dry. Surely I will turn to dust and be blown away by the effort I exert in my life. Please, meet my needs in a way that I can feel your presence and see your hand at work.

In a time of feeling separate from family or community, I might pray:

> Dear Shepherd, I feel like the lost one. I have isolated myself from family and friends by not

telling them the truth, and now I feel outside the group. I long to belong. Can you show me a way to rejoin?

In a time of feeling lost, I might pray:

Dear Shepherd, Find me! Help me find myself! I cannot hear your voice, and I cannot find where you are. Have you left me, or have I left you? Should I run and seek, or should I stand still and wait?

Your turn!

EXERCISE 12—A SINGULAR SALUTATION

Take out your journal. Write down a salutation for God that resonates with your faith and experience. You might choose one from Scripture, from devotional readings or from your life. Then write a series of short prayers (like Jennie's) that reflect the relationship implied from that salutation and your hopes or needs.

For example, if Teresa of Ávila is one of your exemplars of prayer, you might have noticed that in the prayer that we examined in the previous chapter, she uses the verbs "govern," "will" and "are life" to describe God's actions. From this, we can know God as

• Wise Governor

- One Who Wills

- Life and Source of Life

What prayers would come from your heart and experience as a result of using one of those?

We're not suggesting that you use Teresa's example. We're just providing an example of how you have a number of sources from which to draw salutations. Turn back to your journal. What are situations in your life, currently or recurring, that bring you to authentic prayer? Pick three of them and use your chosen salutation to pray about them.

Notice how it felt to write a full (if short) prayer using your new verbs and nouns. If it felt like work, it may be time to remember who is on the other end of this conversation. It's not us. It's the One who knows you absolutely. Take a break from any sense of "working" and consider playing instead.

PLAY BOLDLY

When Brent's family gathers, the games come out.

Monopoly, Apples to Apples, euchre, touch football, or something completely new. Some games have passed away—Trivial Pursuit is long gone. It got to the point where it was the family against me! Playing games is one of the ways we bond. We come closer over food and serious conversations. But playing builds a special bond. And it's something that too many of us forget how to do as we age—something that my kids and grandkids remind me if I start to demur about another round of cutthroat Monopoly.

Playing and *praying* are two words we don't often think of as going together. But in the divine-human relationship, the playing part is what might be missing. As with family and friends, play creates kinship and closeness. When you combine play with pray, you open new closeness to God as you move out of the formal and stuffy and into intimacy. So we're going to paraphrase Martin Luther's famous "Sin boldly" to "Play and pray boldly." With the emphasis on play.

One of Jennie's favorite games in elementary school was Mad Libs. You may have played it too. It involves a story with blanks left in it. One person reads off a list of parts of speech (noun, verb, adjective, adverb) to other players. They shout the first word that comes to their minds. The recorder makes note of the words and then reads the story with the blanks filled in with the words given by people who have no idea what the storyline is. The results are often hilarious.

Mad Libs are still around (there's even an app for them!). We invite you to play our version of them. In doing so, you'll create fresh prayers that use your words. To get the most from this exercise, go with the first words that come to your mind in each scenario. Grab a pencil or pen and write right in this book.

Make this list before you read any further. No peeking!

- salutation for God

- a word or phrase to describe your current state or consuming thought

- action of God that goes with salutation

- thing you are afraid of (may or may not relate to the salutation)

- thing you hope for

- your name

Now, fill in the blanks with your word list, in order, and then read this prayer aloud:

> Dear_____,
>
> Today my heart is full of _____. Because you _____, I am coming to you with what is in my heart. Sometimes I fear _____, but I also hope for _____.
>
> Love,
>
> _____

Here's how Jennie played her Mad-Libs prayer:

- salutation for God: Holy Changer

- a word or phrase to describe your current state or consuming thought: busy and ungrounded

- action of God that goes with salutation: change from scattered to solid

- thing you are afraid of: getting swept away in busyness

- thing you hope for: a sense of calm and center

- your name: Jennie

Here's how Jennie's prayer lib turned out:

> Dear Holy Changer,
>
> Today my heart is full of a sense of busyness and feeling ungrounded. Because you change things from scattered to solid, I am coming to you with what is in my heart. Sometimes I fear that I will be swept away in busyness, but I also hope for a sense of calm and feeling centered.
>
> Love,
> Jennie

Notice that in the "final version," Jennie changed the answers slightly so that the sentences flowed smoothly. The template prayer lib has a rhythm, but it is just a guide. The sample prayer above acknowledges that the holy conversation is happening and that part of the reason it is happening is that the pray-er is confident in an active God. Naming hopes and fears in prayer is part of being authentic. A lot can be packed into a few sentences!

Spend some time with this short fill-in-the-blank exercise. Without thinking too much (since some of us tend to overthink, especially when it comes to our relationship with God), come up with different words. Plug them into the template, and see how the prayers you come up with affect you. Look back at the earlier exercises. Pull images and verbs for God that draw your attention, either positive or negative.

If you feel that the prayer you have created doesn't feel authentic when you offer it in your voice, examine where the dissonance is. Then plug in a word that *works.* Make note if you find yourself just at the edge or outside your comfort zone. In the natural world, the place where forest meets field is called "an edge zone." Such places are often the most vital and thriving with diversity and new life. So don't let any discomfort stop you—just be aware of it.

The next exercise will help you consider the edges of your prayer words and whether they are growing edges or not.

EXERCISE 13—PLAYING A LITTLE MORE BOLDLY

Take out your journal and a pen. Spend some time reflecting on the following questions and write your reflections on them.

1. What was the most "edgy" salutation for God that you have tried so far? What made it feel that way—was it the words or something implied by them?

2. How did the prayers you created feel? Did you read them silently or out loud? If you did both, what differences did you note?

3. What do your prayers bring to the surface about your hopes about God's action and character? About your fears?

4. What word or phrase would you use to characterize your current relationship with God?

Congratulations! If you doubted us earlier in the book when we said everyone is a theologian, you've certainly earned the badge with this exercise. Thinking about God talk and allowing your faith to seek understanding make it so.

PLAYING STILL MORE BOLDLY

Please include me in your work so that I can find ways, with guidance from you and from others who are your vessels and channels, to do the work that I can do and that will contribute to you. Help me figure out what is mine to do. Whether your thing is an experiment, organic growth, a plan or something else, I know that I want to be part of

> it. First, during and last, I am grateful for that chance to have this thing called Life.
>
> **Karie Firoozmand**

Sometimes we find that the names we've used just don't work anymore. We know how this is true in human relationships. Brent used to call his son Tim "Pookie." While playing a soccer game at age five, with Brent shouting encouragement from the sideline, "Pookie" stopped suddenly, looked across the field and yelled, "Call me 'Tim'!" Pookie just didn't work anymore—it works even less now that Tim is in his thirties.

We all have experienced more painful examples as well—like pet names that worked once, but then the relationship fell apart. These things happen in the spiritual realm as well. As we grow and change, we find ourselves offered all sorts of spiritual unfolding that potentially lead us to change our images and salutations for God—if we're honest and authentic. These opportunities come at different times and in response to different circumstances. As we mature in life, and hopefully in faithfulness, things change. It is important and helpful to know what we have left behind and why.

Take a few minutes and think tenderly and honestly as you use your journal to make three lists:

- names and images for God that no longer work for you

- actions attributed to God that do not fit your understanding

- images, salutations and actions for God that you fear may be true but still make you uncomfortable

Some items may appear on multiple lists. That's okay. Let them repeat. This is an exercise in honesty and self-awareness.

Here are the lists that we came up with as we did this:

Images That Didn't Work for Jennie and Brent

- judge

- happy heavenly grandpa

- man in the sky with lightning bolts handy

- celestial Santa Claus

- Mr. Fix-It the Way I Want It Fixed

Actions That Seem Completely Out of Character for Jennie and Brent

- smiting

- walking in the cool of the evening with us

- killing

- punishing harshly

- holding a grudge

  Stuff About God That Jennie and Brent Fear Might Be True

- One who expects more

- that God turns the divine back to some people

- that there is a divine score card I have to see later

- that God is holy wrathful

- that God really is impersonal or uninvolved or uncaring

Once you've made your lists, it's time to do another, more serious prayer lib. Pick

- a salutation for God that does work for you

- two characteristics of God that you believe or have experienced to be true (verbs or adjectives)

- two images or salutations for the Holy that don't work for you or don't make sense

- three actions that seem completely out of character for God

- one thing you might fear is true about God or the relationship between God and humanity

- your name

Make your list. Don't read ahead until you are done. Then drop the words into the blanks in the following prayer. As before, go with what comes out the first time. Afterward, you can make modifications to make it flow more smoothly.

Dear_____,

As our relationship and this conversation deepen, I am strengthened in my certainty that you are _____ and _____. I have at times met others who have referred to or thought of you as _____, which doesn't work for me. Or, they think of you as _____. Sometimes these differences of our understanding make it hard for me to feel compassion and connection to these people. If I follow their understanding of what you are like to see what it means about you, it seems to indicate that you are One who _____, _____ and _____, none of which seem possible given what I have experienced of you. At the same time, I am sometimes afraid that you are actually _____, which is quite scary for me. I wanted to bring these things to our conversation because I want to deepen this relationship, and I want to understand you better. Any help you can offer in increasing my understanding would be a blessing!

Love,

_____

Read your prayer aloud and take some minutes to sit with it. This kind of honesty and vulnerability in prayer about God and your relationship with God is tender work. It deserves time and space.

Here are the results of Jennie doing this exercise:

- a salutation for God that does work for you: Creator

- two characteristics of God that you believe or have experienced to be true: present with me and healer

- two images or salutations for the Holy that don't work for you or don't make sense: judge, punisher

- three actions that seem completely out of character for God: killing, smiting, holding a grudge

- one thing you might fear is true about God or the relationship between God and humanity: that God turns God's back on some

- your name: Jennie

  Dear Creator,

  As our relationship and this conversation deepen, I am strengthened in my certainty that you are the Healer and are present with me. I have at times met others who have referred to or thought of you as judge, which doesn't work for me. Or they think of you as a punisher. Sometimes these differences of our understanding make it hard for me to feel compassion and connection to these people. If I follow their understanding of what you are like to see what it means about you, it seems to indicate that you are one who kills, smites and holds a grudge, none of which seem possible given what I have experienced of you. At the same time, I am sometimes afraid that you actually turn your back on some people, which is quite scary for me. I wanted to bring these things to our conversation because I want to deepen this relationship, and I want to understand you better. Any help you can offer in increasing my understanding would be a blessing!

Love,
Jennie

Having now read your own prayer lib and Jennie's, notice what effect it has on you to acknowledge your uncertainties and to read of another's. Part of being more authentic means being willing to be seen as we pray and live in a spirit that seeks inspiration though is humanly imperfect. Acknowledging and expressing our fears and ignorance do not make us less faithful, nor does it make God love us less. We pray to the One Who Already Knows, and we pray for our own spiritual growth.

EXERCISE 14—SCARY WORDS

If filling in the blanks has primed your pump, it is time to open your journal and write a letter. In it, explain to the Holy the misconceptions you've been exposed to and your feelings about the people who reinforced those ideas. You might also write about the things you fear might be true. Ask for an increase in understanding regarding which of these are true and whether there is new light that might teach you.

What would happen to your relationship with God or your prayer life if what you fear to be true about God is true?

How did the previous prayer lib exercise affect the feelings you have toward persons who have different ideas about God, even ones that are in conflict with your understandings?

What is it like to carry into the conversation with the Holy "some things that need to be cleared up" for the good of the relationship?

Spend some time reading your prayers and your letter to God. Take time for quiet reflection. Make notes of any feelings or insights that arise for you. Revisit those three theological questions introduced in chapter one. They are

- What does _____ say/imply about God?

- What does _____ say/imply about human nature or humanity?

- What does _____ say/imply about the relationship between God and human nature/humanity?

Finally, look at the prayers and lists you have crafted in this chapter. Hold them against the three questions. Journal about any insights that arise, especially about the following:

- Is your approach to prayer any different?

- Are your feelings about prayer any different?

- Have these prayers changed you?

Hopefully, you will answer the last question with a yes! Remember that prayer is a process that changes the pray-er. We've found prayer to be one of our main avenues to transformation. As we learn how to pray in this new way, we find ourselves being welcomed more deeply into God's heart. We also find ourselves being changed into people after God's own heart. When we are close to God's heart, our littleness begins to fade and God's bigness begins to take root. We change, we grow, we become the people God wants us to be.

Let us pray.

5

Hope, Beauty and Depth

ADJECTIVES AND ADVERBS

And he blessed him and said, Blessed (favored with blessings,
made blissful, joyful) be Abram by God Most High,
Possessor and Maker of heaven and earth.

GENESIS 14:19 (AMPLIFIED BIBLE)

A stained-glass voice. A voice that sounds like it is coming from one of the ornate windows in a high cathedral. Have you ever heard one? Brent has. One of his cousins had one. When she prayed, Brent heard some of the most spiritual-sounding prayers a kid ever prayed. They were the kind of prayers that made him afraid to say grace at the dinner table, let alone offer a public prayer at church. His cousin's prayers blossomed with adjectives and adverbs—a figurative floridity of fragrant phrases.

Yet when she finished, while Brent was overwhelmed with a feeling of having heard something special, he was never quite sure exactly what he'd heard. There were so many words, so many descriptors, so many modifiers, that it was hard to remember what had been praised (other than God in general) or asked for or invoked. Her prayers sounded much like what Jesus spoke of in Matthew 6:7: "And when you pray, do not keep on babbling like pagans, for they think they will be heard because of their many words."

One of the things we noticed when we looked at the Lord's Prayer is that Jesus modeled what he meant. The Lord's Prayer is an example of economy of adjectives. In its New Testament original Greek, there's only one true adjective. Its meaning is debatable. That word is *epiousios,* which translates into English as "daily" in regard to bread. This is the only place this word appears in the Bible, and it does not appear in other Greek texts from that era—hence its unclear meaning!

While adjectives have their place in prayer, using too many of them overwhelms the power of the words and sentiments we wish to express. Just look at the Lord's Prayer in the Amplified Bible (a translation that endeavors to expand the meaning of words and verses in the Bible):

> And He said to them, When you pray, say: *Our* Father *Who is in heaven,* hallowed be Your name, Your kingdom come. *Your will be done [held holy and revered] on earth as it is in heaven.*

Give us daily our bread [food for the morrow].

> And forgive us our sins, for we ourselves also forgive everyone who is indebted to us [who has

offended us or done us wrong]. And bring us not into temptation *but rescue us from evil.* (Luke 11:2-4)

That's a lot of amplification! None of it really adds to the prayer. It does make for a good bad example of how to pray, though. It shows how relying on filler words robs our prayers of authenticity and transparency before God.

When Brent teaches writing classes, he often shares Mark Twain's advice to D.W. Bowser about adjectives:

When you catch an adjective, kill it. No, I don't mean utterly, but kill most of them—then the rest will be valuable. They weaken when they are close together. They give strength when they are wide apart. An adjective habit, or a wordy, diffuse, flowery habit, once fastened upon a person, is as hard to get rid of as any other vice.

That's good advice for adjectives in prayer too.

Adjectives are valuable because they can add hope, beauty and depth. The operative word is *can.* Think of the angel's announcement to the shepherds: "I bring you good tidings of great joy, which shall be to all people" (Luke 2:10 KJV). Without adjectives it would be a simple "I have news for people." No zip or wonder there. So adjectives add power when used well.

But first, we have to start by committing grammaricide.

Lord of the springtime, Father of flower, field and fruit, smile on us in these earnest days when the work is heavy and the toil wearisome; lift up our hearts, O God, to the things worthwhile: sunshine and night, the dripping rain, the song of the birds, books and music, and the voices of our friends. Lift up our hearts to these this night and grant us Thy peace. Amen.

W.E.B. DuBois (1868–1963)

EXERCISE 15—MY MODIFIERS

Take out your journal as you ponder some of your usual prayers. Write out one or two of them. Then look them over and underline or circle the following:

- adjectives
- adverbs
- other fillers

Now pray them aloud. Pray them as close to how you normally would. Do you notice any additions—ers, uhs and so on? If so, write them down.

Look over your list and ask:

- Which of these are "habit" words?

- Which of these really help me say what I want to say?

SUBTRACTION

Both of us find that when we pray we enter into mystery. Though we pray via words ushering from our mouths or silently in our minds, we are doing more than speaking or thinking. For us, prayer is not something we're doing. Instead, prayer is a way of being fully present to ourselves and to God in the moment of prayer. We are fully being ourselves. Kathleen Norris describes this state when she says:

> Prayer is not doing, but being. It is not words but the beyond-words experience of coming into the presence of something much greater than oneself. It is an invitation to recognize holiness, and to utter simple words—"Holy, Holy, Holy"—in response. Attentiveness is all; I sometimes think of prayer as a certain quality of attention that comes upon me when I'm busy doing something else.

Prayer as "being" engages body, mind and soul. That's one of the reasons we want to strip our prayers of the adjectives that we rely on too much. We've found that when we do so—in the present moment and with our entire person—we move from idle speech or thought to active attentiveness to divine encounter. Such attentiveness overwhelms us with awe. As Norris points out, the "beyond-words experience" of prayer eliminates all that is extraneous and distracting. We are brought to a place where the simplest language suffices to utter the longings and feelings of our souls.

That's the reason the first step in giving our words power is stripping them down—starting with the adjectives. Subtraction helps us pray prayers that are alive as we come before the Lord of life with our prayers. Words filled with power give life and juicyness to our prayers. Our prayers need—and deserve—juice, both in the electrical sense and the thirst quenching sense. When we've stripped our prayers to words from our deepest parts and reveal our longings, hopes, praise, adoration and awe, then we feel their power. We've had moments of such prayer. They're momentary glimpses into eternity with our soul's desires for wholeness and communion with God completely fulfilled.

EXERCISE 16—SUBTRACTION

Take a moment to look over the adjectives you came up with in the previous exercise. Remember, as you look them over, there's nothing wrong with adjectives—so long as they are authentic. Are they real? Are they words you use at times other than prayer? Or are they part of your mental box of God words—pulled out only when you pray? If the answer to that last question is yes, then you may want to excise them from your prayer life—at least for a while.

Eliminating such words helps us cultivate prayer as a way of being in the vitality and authenticity of our daily life.

USUALLY WEAK

We often say that adverbs should generally be avoided (*generally* being an adverb). That's because in writing they're usually (wink) considered weak words. They tell but don't show. Psalm 63 gives us a good example. Though we're loath to ... um ... criticize Scripture, the first verse starts off just a little lame. "You, God, are my God, earnestly I seek you." "Earnestly" tells but doesn't show. What does "earnestly" look like?

The psalmist quickly corrects his telling and moves to showing—"I thirst for you, my whole being longs for you, in a dry and parched land where there is no water." Okay, now there's an image we can get our bodies, minds, and souls around.

In the verses that follow, there's more showing. There are few adjectives and fewer adverbs.

> I thirst for you,
> my whole being longs for you,
> in a dry and parched land
> where there is no water.
> I have seen you in the sanctuary
> and beheld your power and your glory.
> Because your love is better than life,

my lips will glorify you.
I will praise you as long as I live,
and in your name I will lift up my hands.
I will be fully satisfied as with the richest of
 foods;
with singing lips my mouth will praise you.

Take a few moments and read this psalm aloud. Notice your intonations. Inflections. How it feels on your tongue. In your head. In your heart. When you read these words, do you get a sense of being dry and parched? How is the psalmist's description of "a dry and parched land" more powerful than just saying "thirstily"? Notice the power this prayer generates.

As we thought about the prayer adverbs we use, we came up with

- cautiously

- hopefully

- curiously

- thirstily

- prayerfully

- gratefully

- humbly

Since we both had the adverb *prayerfully* on our list, we wondered: What does it look like to approach God prayerfully? Is it about physical posture?

The prayer that came out of our musings is:

> Regal God—as your servant in the Scriptures, I prostrate myself before you. You are my Lord, know my needs and alone can answer them. I ask your grace and favor. Amen.

Then we played with *curiously.* Our playful prayer came out:

> God of Wonder and Mystery—I wonder what's in store? What blessings and challenges do you have for me? How will this day unfold as I try my best to follow your way? My heart and soul are open to adventure, so long as you are with me. AMEN!

EXERCISE 17—AVOIDING EARNESTLY AND ALL THE OTHER LEES

List your adverbs on a sheet of paper or in your journal. Pick one and write a prayer that does not use it but instead uses a description of what that word means to you. What does it mean to pray in the way your adverb describes? Show how you feel—don't tell.

Then mentally "set aside" your list. Put the words on it away for a while. Not because they're bad words, but because you want to pray "beyond-words" in the same way the psalmist did.

JUST-IFYINGOUR PRAYERS

While Facebooking one day, Brent came across the "Register of Attendance" image.

While the attendance to offering ratio would be the concern of many ministers, the thing that caught Brent's attention was the "Times the Word 'Just' Was Used in Our Prayers."

When I saw that picture, I had a sort of flashback to my days as a Young Life leader. Prayers back then seemed filled with "justs" and "just reallys." As someone who's prone to picking up the accents and idioms of the friends I hang around with, I know some of the prayers that came out of my mouth were along the lines of "Lord, we JUST pray that you would JUST like, JUST really JUST totally..."

"Just" what was it that I "just" wanted God to do or hear???

Whatever it was Brent wanted, all the "justs" weren't helping him be clear about it. As E.M. Bounds once said, "Our praying, however, needs to be pressed and pursued with an energy that never tires, a persistency which will not be denied, and a courage which never fails." Such energetic, persistent, courageous praying doesn't allow itself to be burdened with lazy words.

Imagine for a moment that Jesus walks into the room and says, "Let's talk. Tell me what's on your heart." After you got over the initial shock (if you did!), extraneous words would fall by the wayside. There would be no "justs" or other verbal tics we too often rely on. We need to use words that live and breathe and come from our souls. Jesus has walked into the room!

EXERCISE 18—IMPLICATIONS

Think about the adjectives, adverbs and other fillers you use when you pray. They may be words you listed earlier or they might be ones that are bubbling up for you now. You might want to look over your journal. Examine them in the light of the three theological questions introduced in chapter one. Pick an adjective, adverb or filler word and ask:

• What does *this word* say/imply about God?

- What does *this word* say/imply about human nature or humanity?

- What does *this word* say/imply about the relationship between God and human nature/humanity?

Journal about any insights that arise.

ADDITION

So why not just eliminate all adjectives, adverbs and other qualifiers? Wouldn't that be easiest? Maybe, but we want to use such words and phrases when they add hope, beauty and depth. Let's look again at Psalm 63.

> I have seen you in the sanctuary
> and beheld your power and your glory.
> Because your love is better than life,
> my lips will glorify you.
> I will praise you as long as I live,
> and in your name I will lift up my hands.
> I will be fully satisfied as with the richest of
> foods;
> with singing lips my mouth will praise you.
> (vv.2-5)

Notice that the only adjectives used "punch up" the meanings. Not just "food" but "the richest of food" and not just "lips" but "singing lips." "Fully" modifies "satisfied" for further wow factor. These words each add beauty, hope and depth.

Likewise, a classic prayer of St. Augustine uses modifiers to profound effect.

> Watch, dear Lord,
> with those who wake, or watch, or weep tonight,
> and give Your angels charge over those who sleep.
> Tend Your sick ones, O Lord Christ.
> Rest Your weary ones.
> Bless Your dying ones.
> Soothe Your suffering ones.
> Pity Your afflicted ones.
> Shield Your joyous ones.
> And all for Your Love's sake.
>
> Amen.

This prayer begins not just with "Lord" but with "dear Lord." That short phrase engenders feelings of tenderness along with respectful acknowledgment of the power and rank of the divine. The prayer ends with "Your Love's sake" not just "love's sake." It reminds us that all love is rooted in and grows from God's love for us. Likewise, the words "sick," "weary," "suffering," "afflicted" and "joyous" each paint images of the persons for whom we're praying. Indeed, those words may help us call to mind those in our lives whom we know to be sick, weary, suffering, afflicted or joyous. Using universal adjectives like these call to mind specific people we know and care about—but whom we might intentionally not think of if we merely prayed

> Watch, Lord,
> all for love's sake.

> Amen.

The above "abridged" version of Augustine's prayer is a fine prayer, if it comes from our hearts. But by paying attention to the adjectives and other modifiers, it's easy to see how much deeper and richer the original version is. It takes us to a place closer to the heart of God and the desires of our souls than does the shorter prayer.

EXERCISE 19—GROWING OUR PRAYERS

Besides adding hope and beauty, using the right words—words that come from deep within us and are more than fillers—also adds depth and nuance to our prayers. Now that you've put together a list of words that you don't want to use, begin to think of words that you do want to use to describe God's attributes. How does this list work for you?

> Kind
> Fierce
> Vulnerable
> Friendly
> Gracious

Wonderful
Selfless
Patient
Committed
Habitable
Safe
Wondrous
Happy
Communicative
Jealous
Hospitable
Abundant

What words would you add to deepen your list? You might want to expand the list to include words you don't currently use. Are they words you normally use in everyday conversation? You might want to add words that you use when talking to someone you love deeply. What would it mean to use such intimate language in prayer? Use a modification of the three questions to help you go deeper.

- What word or phrase can help me connect more deeply to what I believe about God?

- What word or phrase can help me connect more deeply to what I believe about myself and/or human nature or humanity?

- What word or phrase can help me connect more deeply to what I believe about the relationship between God and human nature/humanity?

Please give me courage and confidence. Please help me to say the things that need to be said and avoid saying the things that don't. Please calm my nerves and give me peace. Thank you for the many blessings and opportunities you have given me. Thank you for opening the right doors and closing the wrong ones. I pray that what is meant to be will be. I pray that my impact will be a positive one, today and every day. Thank you for your guidance and love. Amen.

Sarah Rejoice Brown

METAPHORS THAT MEAN MORE

We Quakers have many metaphors for Jesus or God or the Holy Spirit. Light, Seed and Inward Light are just some of them. Metaphors in the life of the spirit are nothing new. Scripture is filled with them: Father, rock, bread of life, breath, wind, potter and, of course, the familiar shepherd. When we look at the first four verses of the Twenty-Third Psalm, we see that the shepherd image there paints a picture of God that is far different from many other Old Testament understandings. This is not God as warrior king—wrathful, jealous and more. "Shepherd" may have opened up a new way of seeing for those who heard this psalm for the first time.

David was not the only saint to use metaphor. Many of the saints—Brother Lawrence, St. Teresa and Julian of Norwich, for example—used metaphor to deepen their understanding of God and their prayers. Julian of Norwich's "Mother Jesus" especially takes an image of Jesus and tilts it so that we see Jesus afresh. "Mother God" may be an image that jars some of us, but Jesus as mother requires even more wrestling. After all, how can the man Jesus be our mother?

Throughout time, pray-ers like Julian and prayers like hers have used the images of their time to move beyond contemporary images of the divine and go more deeply into the personal. We can do the same today by thinking about what metaphors we can apply.

A metaphor for God that has been central for Jennie in recent years is water. It works for her because of water's variable forms. God's love sometimes seems as deep as an apparently bottomless well. At other times, God's presence startles Jennie to awareness like splooshy drops of water falling on an otherwise dry day. She may experience an inner flow or a deep spring of connection with God while engaged in contemplative practices. Conversely, she may also have a parched sense that comes with her perception of God's absence.

With so many possible iterations of God's presence as water, the prayer possibilities are nearly endless when one taps into the vocabulary of words related to the metaphor. For water, God might be

- ocean
- river
- current
- lake
- deeps
- rain
- dew

The desire for God might be

- the urge to swim
- thirst
- dry skin
- being too hot
- being too cold

The person in prayer might see herself as

- a boat
- an empty cup
- a fish who does not even grasp the idea of the water that surrounds it

Using the water metaphor in times of fear might lead us to pray:

Boundless Ocean, upon which all of us on earth stand, whether we know it or not, take me to the still waters beneath the roiling surface of my life.

In times of sadness or absence, that metaphor could find us praying:

Loving God, fill the dryness of my perception with your gentle dew. I have lost my way, and do not trust that I can survive without the encouragement of your flow.

In times of celebration, if we stay with the water metaphor, we might pray:

Filler of my cup, I am overflowing with awareness of your grace. Thank you for causing me to flourish!

In these examples, the metaphor of water implies that God is everywhere and in diverse forms. It also indicates that humanity needs God, as we need water, for our basic needs in daily life—to drink, to grow food, to wash. The relationship between God and humanity can be understood to be one of a built-in desire for God. It could also be a terror if we fear being swept away when we yield control to the oceanic One.

Water is a metaphor that works for us. It may not work for you. The next exercise will help you get in touch with metaphors that mean something to you.

EXERCISE 20—PRAYING METAPHORICALLY

As you think about your experience of God, what images come to mind that could serve as metaphors? To what metaphors do your thoughts take you?

Don't overthink it. Try to put your brain in neutral and instead live out of your soul and heart and feelings. You might want to flip through your journal and look at some of the images that you came up with in earlier exercises. Grow them into fuller images, more complete metaphors. If you need a jumpstart, consider completing the sentence "God is like..." and see what comes up. Then drop the comparison language of "like" and see if the metaphor can stand on its own. As you come up with a metaphor that feels especially close to your heart, ask, "Why is this metaphor important to me now?" Then use it to construct a prayer that grows out from it.

Write your prayer. That way you can make each word count and make sure that you keep to the metaphor (as David did in Psalm 23). Let your prayer flow from your imagination and soul.

As you look over your prayer, ask:

• How does this metaphor help me see God in a fresh, new way?

- How does this metaphor help me see myself in soul-breaking-open ways?

- Does this metaphor help me see the relationship between God and myself the way my heart wishes it to be?

The important thing regarding adjectives, adverbs, metaphors and other creative words is that they need to be authentic. They need to come from our hearts. Our experience. Our culture. Our lives. They need to be more than fillers. Perhaps that's why early twentieth-century Catholic spiritual director Dom Chapman taught, "Pray as you can, not as you can't. Take yourself as you find yourself; start from that." That's good advice. We think, "Pray from your heart and imagination, not your rational, judging mind" would be equally good.

Trust your heart and soul to lead you to the adjectives, adverbs and metaphors that speak to and from the deepest part of you. Trust them to take you nearer to God. Then bow your head, lift your heart and pray them.

6

Unpacking Meaning

SHARED LANGUAGE AND AUTHENTIC PRAYER

So what shall I do? I will pray with my spirit,
but I will also pray with my understanding.

1 CORINTHIANS 14:15

We wanted to be better pray-ers. That's one reason this book came into being—to help us move deeply into a life of soul-filling, spirit-renewing prayer. At times we've thought, wouldn't it have been great to sit at Jesus' feet and learn how to pray? What better prayer teacher could we have than Jesus?

That's something the disciples knew. That's why they begged, "Lord, teach us to pray" (Luke 11:1). As the disciples listened, they heard the power of Jesus' prayer—not just in the words but also in the spirit and meaning behind them. There was something exceptional about Jesus' praying. It was intimate. Forceful. Heartfelt. Direct. Passionate. Perhaps they recognized that this was the kind of prayer that, as Joan Chittister says, "concentrates the mind and enlarges the soul." It was the type of prayer they wished to pray. It's the type of prayer we all long for—to concentrate our minds and enlarge our souls.

It's not that we, or the disciples, don't know how to pray. We do and they did. They had grown up seeing their fathers and grandfathers standing in synagogue praying. They, like Jesus, prayed the *Sh'ma Yisrael* of their time:

> Hear, O Israel: The Lord our God, the Lord is one. Love the Lord your God with all your heart and with all your soul and with all your strength. These commandments that I give you today are to be on your hearts. Impress them on your children. Talk about them when you sit at home and when you walk along the road, when you lie down and when you get up. Tie them as symbols on your hands and bind them on your foreheads. Write them on the doorframes of your houses and on your gates.

As we've shared, we've had prayers and praying examples throughout our lives too. You may have had, as well.

When they listened to Jesus praying, though, their ears and hearts heard something different about his prayers compared to their own. When we read of Jesus' prayers, we encounter something that resounds in the deepest part of our spirits. Jesus' praying is a window, opening to a vista of what real prayer can be.

Our next exercise will help us to pray as Jesus prayed.

EXERCISE 21—LEARNING FROM JESUS

Imagine for a few minutes that you were one of the women or men in that first-century company of the committed. How do you envision Jesus' prayers affecting you? What about them would move you to desire to pray as he did—so much that you would cry out with the others, "Lord, teach me to pray!"?

Take out your Bible and look at some of Jesus' prayers. Ones you might want to pay particular attention to are Matthew 11:25-26; Luke 22:32, 41-44; John 11:41-42; and John 17:1-26. As you look at these prayers, reflect on what they say about Jesus' understanding of the nature of prayer. Why did he pray the way he did? What made his prayers "real"?

Eternal God, let thy Spirit inspire and guide us. Thy will be done.

Give us the strength to fulfill our task without selfishness, slothfulness or cowardice.

Give us the strength to withstand temptations, and to forgive others as we would wish them freely to forgive us.

Enable us to repay those who offend us only by redoubling our endeavors never to offend others.

Eternal God, we will listen to thy call and obey it in order that we may hear it ever more clearly.

Give us the honesty to examine our own acts and thoughts as scrupulously and severely as those of other people.

Deliver us from the fanaticism and pride which prevent us from welcoming truth even when it comes through the teaching and experience of others.

Give us the calm assurance that thou thyself wilt know how to reveal thy truth and righteousness to others even as we believe that thou hast in measure revealed them to us.

Teach us compassion and enable us to make a real effort to relieve the sufferings of others.

Give us the quiet courage needed in all circumstances, and natural to whoever has consecrated his life to thee.

At the highest level of existence where man and woman meet one another, let there be above all a passionate regard for the true values of life, for thy truth and thy love above all.

Do not let any defeat, and fall or backsliding ever separate us from thee; in the midst of all our weakness let thy love take hold of us and little by little lift us up to thee.

Pierre Ceresole (1879–1945)

Next, as you think about your prayers today, what would help you pray in the same way Jesus did?

Take your journal and write down three to five things you think might help you to pray as Jesus did.

LORD, TEACH US TO PRAY

Many of us know the Lord's Prayer so well that we don't see it for the new example of prayer that the disciples did. It was so fresh compared to the formal prayers they were used to praying that certainly they had to take it apart, examine the words and their meanings, look at it carefully for nuance and fit with their lives before it could become a model for their everyday praying. Yet it was the prayer Jesus gave when asked to teach prayer to his beloved followers.

Think about it. Jesus introduces them to a type of praying that blows their prayer norms around like so many falling leaves in an autumn wind. But such, as Jesus tells them (John 3:8), is the way of the Spirit.

We're not going to parse the various words and phrases of the Lord's Prayer (there are many fine books that do that). As writer Kayla McClurg of the Church of the Savior points out:

> The outline for prayer that Jesus gives is simple: honor God, ask for God's ways to come into being among us and for our daily needs to be met (which is how we know God's ways are among us), forgive ourselves and others, and ask for the

strength to resist the temptations that can tug us away from all of this.

Rather, we want to share some of the things we learned as we studied this prayer. What we saw changed our praying in some of the same ways the disciples probably found their praying being changed.

One of the first things about Jesus' prayers that the disciples had to unpack was when and where to pray. In the first century, many of Judaism's prayers were offered at set times or occasions and places. Jesus, however, seemed to be praying all the time. He prayed at places far from the usual synagogue or religious service. The Bible tells us that he prayed alone, in the wilderness, in the Garden of Gethsemane, and many other times and places.

As we thought about the places and times we prayed, we found that we had some patterns: prayers before meals at home, nighttime prayers using the examen and prayers during private devotions. Ours in some ways modeled Jesus'—more private prayers than public ones. It's a pattern, perhaps, that we've gotten locked into. Praying in public is not something we often do—unless we're leading a workshop, preaching somewhere, praying aloud with spiritual direction clients or at family Thanksgiving.

As we looked at when Jesus taught the disciples to pray, we noticed that, unlike our tendency to pray primarily in private, this private prayer stretched all their cultural and religious boundaries. Maybe almost to the breaking point. Which is not a bad thing. We all need to be stretched. Challenged. Reshaped. Changed. If, that is, we want to pray authentically.

So if you primarily pray private prayers, one way of stretching is to pray publicly. As an introvert, Brent finds this idea particularly challenging.

> *While I find Norman Rockwell's* Saying Grace *touching, this famous illustration of a grandmother and grandson bowed in prayer in a restaurant makes me a little nervous. Not that I'm ashamed to pray, but the idea of people observing me doing so makes me nervous. I don't want to be the focus of attention like the woman and child in the painting are. Even if I was praying silently.*

For that reason alone, praying over his burger at Steak and Shake might be exactly what Brent needs to do to stretch himself.

It's easy to review our words as we think about how we pray. Especially if we want to pray like Jesus. But Jesus' teaching on prayer goes deeper than words. He teaches us to look at our prayer habits—words, times, places. So we do well to pay attention not just to what Jesus prayed, but how and where he prayed. Jesus' teachings on prayer—both by example and in his words – show that each act of prayer draws life into us as we share with the One who wants the best for us.

UNPACKING

Still, since this is, after all, a book about prayer and language, let's return to the words Jesus used in the Lord's Prayer. Radio host Krista Tippet of radio's *On Being* says, "The words we choose color the way we think and see. They shape the way we move through the world—and move us towards others, or away." When we read Tippet's words, we remember just how strongly words influence how we think, feel and sense our relationship with God, others and this world as we move through it. That's why, since we have become so familiar with the Lord's Prayer that we are unable to hear it or speak it in a meaningful way, we can use some variations of it to help us discover renewed meaning.

With Scripture. One way to do that is, of course, to read the familiar passage in a translation that is new to us. New language helps us think in new ways. Fresh words unlock meanings that are fresh to us. They may have been there all along, but somehow we have missed them. Seeing Scripture again for the first time opens a clean window, giving us a glimpse into that which we have missed because we've seen through a glass darkly.

For example, J.B. Phillips's translation has the prayer beginning with

> Our Heavenly Father, may your name be honoured; May your kingdom come, and your will

be done on earth as it is in heaven. (Matthew 6:9-10 *The New Testament in Modern English)*

How do those words differ from the ones you normally use? Or are they so close to what you're used to that there is nothing jarring or different or soul-eye opening?

Perhaps the way *The Message* starts—"Our Father in heaven, Reveal who you are. Set the world right; Do what's best—as above, so below" (Matthew 6:9-10)—will provide an original look at this prayer for you.

As you read different versions of this (or any) prayer, look for slightly new, but significant, takes on the meaning of the prayer. Do the opening sentences change or challenge your thinking about this known-by-heart-and-soul prayer that you may have prayed for years?

With music. Using music is another way to open up new meaning. Albert Hay Malotte's 1935 version of the Lord's Prayer is one of the most recognizable musical representations of this prayer. It's been performed by everybody from church soloists in congregations big and small to Frank Sinatra and the Mormon Tabernacle Choir. But there are other versions of the Lord's Prayer, as well. John Michael Talbot's is as spare as it is moving. Mbongeni Ngema's arrangement from the play and Whoopi Goldberg film *Sarafina! The Sound of Freedom* is joyous with a distinctive South African feel. That's not surprising since Ngema is a South African lyricist and composer. Brent sometimes uses a musical version of the Lord's Prayer by musician and writer John Fischer, whom he met in college. It begins

> Holy Father hear our prayer
> Keep us always in Your care
> May Your kingdom come to us
> And may we learn how to trust

With visual arts. In addition to music, think of tools you can use to help you enliven the common prayers of your life and fill them with new meaning. Are you attuned to the visual arts? If so, do an Internet search for "Lord's prayer art." Hundreds of images will appear, from the schlocky to the profound. Some will have fine art backgrounds. Others will be graphic representations with the feel of an illuminated manuscript. As you look at them, ask yourself if the layout with art releases understandings you had not thought of.

Or you could try doing something completely original and use your creativity to unlock new meanings of this venerable prayer. As we mentioned earlier, Brent often does what he calls "praying with my camera." He uses his Nikon to capture images of God through the viewfinder. You don't need a Nikon; you can use your smartphone's camera. Pull it out and spend some time engaging in your own praying with a camera.

Look around your world for images that capture the aha of the Lord's Prayer for you.

With literary arts. Perhaps the literary arts speak to you more than do those visual or musical. If that's the case, spend some time with poetic versions of this prayer. Classic versions include ones by John Bowring:

> O thou high and holy One!
> Who in heaven hast fixed Thy throne,
> Whom we God and Father call—
> Father! dearest name of all;

John Bunyan's version is another classic:

> Our Father which in heaven art,
> Thy name be always hallowed;
> Thy kingdom come, thy will be done;
> Thy heavenly path be followed.

Our next exercise invites you to use some of these ways of unpacking.

EXERCISE 22—UNPACKING

Pick a translation of the Lord's Prayer that is familiar or interesting to you. See if you can imagine singing the prayer words, or a modified version of them, to a favorite song tune. Does the prayer feel like it needs a classical backdrop or a slow country ballad? Can you imagine a jaunty dance number or more of a meditative instrumental number?

Notice and reflect on the chance to add a creative musical twist to a familiar prayer. Did you feel free to add music? Did your attitude about your prayer shift when considering music? Did you encounter resistance or feel that you could only use a specific kind of music?

If you want to go a step further with your unpacking, consider creating a slide show of images. You could either use clips from the Internet or photos you have taken that capture the essence of the prayer. If you found music that makes your prayer feel authentic, you might have the slide show synched with the music. Then you could use it as a highly personalized meditative prayer experience.

CRAFTING

Another way we've discovered to find fresh meaning in familiar prayers is to craft our own versions of them. This includes the Lord's Prayer. You may think, as we did, *Who am I to try toimprove on the Lord's Prayer?* Well, you are a creative being acting out one aspect of your own incarnation. We are made in the image of God. Part of the *imago Dei* means that we are creative and imaginative creatures who delight in new things. Besides, Jesus did not command, "Use these exact words."

When we began practicing how to make our own version of the Lord's Prayer, we looked for the words and phrases that captured all its elements:

- praise

- worship

- submission to divine will

- forgiveness for others as well as ourselves

- supplication for our needs

We began by making lists of words or phrases that captured the essence of the prayer for us. The hard part was shushing our internal editors. They kept saying things such as *Well, if I prayed that aloud at church next Sunday, the Right Reverend Doctor High-church would haul me before a canonical counsel before I got out of the sanctuary* or *Sister Bertha Mae would have a heart attack!* We had to remember that this prayer was not for them. It was for us. For our edification and creative release. We wanted to pray in our own words as a way to go deeper into communion with the great Lover of Our Souls. So we listened solely to the words of the Spirit moving within us. As it says in Romans 8:26, "The Spirit helps us in our weakness. We do not know what we ought to pray for, but the Spirit himself intercedes for us through wordless groans."

We found that crafting (or recasting) the Lord's Prayer this way made it personal. It became a prayer from our very soul—calling us deeper into a life that is transformational, incarnational and closer to God than we'd ever been. Maybe the next exercise will help you do just that too.

EXERCISE 23—THE (INSERT YOUR NAME)'S PRAYER

Imagine, for a moment, that a dear friend comes up to you and pleads, "Teach me to pray." After the initial shock—and many disclaimers about how you are unworthy—what prayer would you teach them? What words and phrases from your experience would you use? Not just words that feel easy and familiar, but words that you've found from culture and your faith that feel genuine. Think of the form that Jesus used.

- a salutation

- a phrase honoring God

- asking for God's ways to be realized

- requesting our daily needs to be met

- appealing for forgiveness and an attitude of forgiving

- assistance in resisting temptation

- closing

To give you an idea of how to do this, here's what Brent came up with:

- a salutation: Loving God

- a phrase honoring God: Great is the way you care for your people and all creation

- asking for God's ways to be realized: Let your ways of love become a part of all of human experience

- requesting our daily needs to be met: The needs of this world are great; please meet them for all people out of your love and grace

- appealing for forgiveness and an attitude of forgiving: Teach us to drop our petty remembrances of others' offenses toward us in the same way you practice holy forgetfulness of our errors

- assistance in resisting temptation: The world offers much to entice us away from the life of faith, help us resist those offers

- closing: You have the power to do all the things we request, both here and now, and for all time and eternity

With a bit of editing for flow, here's how Brent's prayer came out:

Loving God, great is the way you care for your people and all creation. Let your ways of love become a part of all of human experience. The needs of this world are great, please meet them for us and all people out of your love and grace and the actions you teach us. Teach us how to drop our petty remembrances of others' offenses toward us in the same way you practice holy forgetfulness toward us. The world tries hard to entice us away from the life of faith, help us resist those offers. You have the power to do all the things we request, both here and now, and for all time and eternity. So be it.

Now it's your turn.

UNCOMFORTABLE WORDS

Are your prayers always "nice"? We have to admit that ours often are. To pray "not nice" prayers is scary—and seems a bit dangerous. Yet praying authentically is not about always using comfortable, easy, or nice words and phrases. Especially when we're not feeling comfortable, easy or nice.

Using uncomfortable words at times seems counterintuitive to many of us. Jennie, when she was a child, thought that prayer was about getting God closer to her or to whomever she was praying for. She saw her prayers as a sort of sending up flares to that busy lightning-bolt-wielding old guy to catch his notice. Nice seemed the best way to accomplish that.

But the truth is that the words our souls want to use may not be comfortable, nice words. That's okay, because the object of prayer is not our comfort. Rather, it is connection. It is about getting us closer to God.

Getting us closer to God is about moving us nearer to God's heart and thereby moving us closer to the people we were created to be. When we pray in such an authentic way, we may find ourselves filled with hope and comfort, even if the prayers are uncomfortable in the uttering.

The Bible is filled with prayers that are salted with uncomfortable words or thoughts. While the saintliness and patience of Job have acquired a mythic quality, they are that—mythic. Job was faithful and saintly but hardly patient. Just look at this prayer:

> I say to God: Do not declare me guilty,
> but tell me what charges you have against me.
> Does it please you to oppress me,
> to spurn the work of your hands,
> while you smile on the plans of the wicked?
> Do you have eyes of flesh?
> Do you see as a mortal sees? (Job 10:2-4)

Um, hardly the words of a patient man.

Yet the words are true. They pour out as Job's lifeblood. He is unafraid to use them. Perhaps that's because he's at the near end to despair. But more likely it is because of the sort of man Job was—a person of integrity whose life reflected the words he prayed and whose words reflected his true spiritual state. While such prayers may make us uncomfortable, they do so because they are authentic cries from the depths of the heart. They show us, too, that it is okay to stop playing it safe in our relationship with God.

Of course, we might think, *Well, that's okay for Job to talk that way to God. He had some pretty good grievances. However, he does come across, justifiably perhaps, as a bit of a whiner.* But Job's not the only biblical character that addresses God as directly and honestly as we would address our spouse or best friend when they've let us down (not that Brent or Jennie's spouses ever do!).

The psalmists often praise God as a being of justice and mercy. But when they look at injustice, they begin wondering. Many is the psalm that asks, basically, "What's going on here?"

> How long, Lord? Will you forget me forever?
> How long will you hide your face from me?
> How long must I wrestle with my thoughts
> and day after day have sorrow in my heart?
> How long will my enemy triumph over me?
> Look on me and answer, Lord my God. (Psalm 13:1-3)

"Look on me and answer." That's a pretty direct demand, even in the sedate language of the New International Version. *The Message* renders that last verse "Take a good look at me."

Pray-ers in the Bible—the authentic, truthful ones—risk nagging God in plain language. Language using hard words, at times. Uncomfortable language. Even Jonah—the great malingerer who does God's will only after spending time in solitude in the belly of a great fish—lets God "have it" when the results aren't quite what he hoped (he thought God let the people of

Nineveh off too easy). "Isn't this what I said, Lord, when I was still at home? That is what I tried to forestall by fleeing to Tarshish" (Jonah 4:2).

Do we chance praying with this kind of audacity and intimacy?

Our friend Katherine did. Once, when she had felt what she considered a clear leading from God to attend seminary and had proceeded to change her life to do that, everything went awry. And so she had words with God. Words that poured out of her anguish and upset. She says, "I stood in my bedroom and yelled at the ceiling—toward God. I pulled out the Bible, pointed at different verses and said things like, 'Well, what about this promise and that promise?'"

She ranted and raved and didn't mince any words. And then, spent, she felt overcome with a sense of peace and intimacy with God that she had not felt in a long time. No, everything wasn't instantly better. But her honesty and uncomfortable words took her relationship with God to a deeper level.

> God, you'd better be with me in this!
>
> **Ashley Wilcox**

Our relationship with the divine needs to be such that we can say what's truly on our hearts and in our souls, even when it's confrontational and direct. Jesus demanded, "My God, my God, why have you forsaken me?" (Matthew 27:46). Our spiritual ancestor Jacob wrestled with God. Literally. Perhaps it's time for you to go to the mat with God. That's the sort of relationship with the Holy we are called into. To not pray with such fervor in the face of our discomfort and disappointment is to deny ourselves a transforming relationship with God. Such prayer changes us. It makes us transparent to God—and ourselves. Dare we be such?

EXERCISE 24—A "BAD" WORDS PRAYER

Make a list of true but uncomfortable words and phrases. It needs to be a list of words that you rarely use in prayer. Or better yet, words and phrases you can't imagine using! Remember that earlier exercise having you list words and attributes that you could never ever attribute to God? Maybe now is the time to pull them out and use them. It's time to leave your "faith manners" on the shelf by the door and pray without filters, at the edge of your comfort, or colorfully.

Don't be fearful of sounding whiny or petty. True, your complaints may not have the weight of Job's (you might still have your health and cattle), but your trials are as real to you as Job's were to him.

Authentic, meaningful, strong and courageous prayer words help us stand before God spiritually naked and soulfully transparent. Authentic, meaningful, strong and courageous prayer words enable us to embrace our incarnating, becoming agents of faithful responsiveness in our end of the holy conversation. That's why we've spent all this time opening up our spiritual baggage and taking a good look at the words, images, beliefs and lenses of all types. We want to give fresh voice to the inarticulate speech of our souls. That is our desire. Our hope.

Hear our prayer, nice or not, O Lord.

7

Jesus, the Word of God, and Our Words

The Word became flesh and made his dwelling among us.

JOHN 1:14

Are you more of a crucifixion person or a resurrection person?" That's what participants were asked at a workshop Jennie was attending. When it was her turn Jennie responded, "Well, actually, I'm more of an incarnation person."

> *My answer surprised me. I had never considered aligning myself with a stage in the Passion story. Somehow, though, the teacher's question and my answer located the center of my identity as a spiritual being. That's because, for me incarnation, in part, means using my life and being to manifest the glimpse I've been given of God's Way for the world. Incarnation is about closing the gap between what is and what could be.*

As we talked about Jennie's understanding of incarnation, we realized that the idea of closing the gap is true for incarnational prayer, as well. That's because, as we understand it, incarnation describes both the central historical event that kicked off the Christian movement *and* the ongoing task of the disciples of Jesus.

As Michael Spenser says, "Without the incarnation, Christianity isn't even a very good story, and most sadly, it means nothing. 'Be nice to one another' is not a message that can give my life meaning, assure me of love beyond brokenness, and break open the dark doors of death with the key of hope." We all enjoy a good story, and we want our lives to tell one—a story that is good, in all the best senses of that word. We want our prayers to tell a good story too. After all, many of our best conversations are in story forms, so it's natural that prayer should be a story.

While *incarnation* is not a word that tends to make its way into daily conversation ("Say, Frank, I've been meaning to ask you, what do you think about the incarnation?"), it is central to Christian faith. We don't have any intention of getting into the mystery and dogmatic distinctions of the incarnation here. For our purpose of growing deeper in authentic prayer, the incarnation of Jesus describes the understanding from the Gospels that the pre-existing Word became manifest in human history as Jesus. We know, and honor, that Christians hold varying understandings of the incarnation. But the one thing about the incarnation all Christians agree on is that God's nature is revealed as never before in the life and teachings of Jesus of Nazareth. That revelation helps us as we pray because the incarnation shows us in a very real, human way the personality of the person to whom we pray.

Likewise, as part of the ongoing task of the disciples of Jesus, incarnation has special relevance to our prayer. Incarnational prayer was initiated by Jesus when he gathered the first community of disciples to himself. As Jesus brings them together, he doesn't just teach them. No, he sends them out to do his work, and more.

> I ask for daily bread, but not for wealth, lest I forget the poor.
>
> I ask for strength, but not for power, lest I despise the meek.
>
> I ask for wisdom, but not for learning, lest I scorn the simple.
>
> I ask for a clean name, but not for fame, lest I condemn the lowly.
>
> I ask for peace of mind, but not for idle hours, lest I fail to hearken to the call of duty.
>
> **Inazo Nitobe (1862–1933)**

But it wasn't just for them. As Jesus told Philip, "Very truly I tell you, whoever believes in me will do the works I have been doing, and they will do even greater things than these." The mystical body of Christ spans time and geography. It is comprised of the faithful. Us. We're under Christ's leadership, present today in the works of the Holy Spirit, the sacraments, Scripture and in mystical encounters in daily life. The diverse yet faithful body of believers seeks to live in response to the teachings of Christ as we understand them.

These two understandings of incarnation (that of Jesus, and of the body of Christ comprised of the faithful after the resurrection) are the heart of all Christian spirituality and its practices. Including prayer. For us, both dimensions of the incarnation help us understand the purpose and nature of prayer. Since we both affirm the revelation of God's love in the human life of Jesus and the life-giving metaphor of the body of Christ as the community of faithful, we see prayer as conversation in which we can be vulnerable and honest in our communication and also wait expectantly to hear from God.

EXERCISE 25—DISCIPLESHIP AS LISTENING

Discipling is one of many terms used to describe adult spiritual formation in contemporary congregations. For a few moments, consider the earlier definition of a disciple. A disciple is one who is called and taught by Jesus, the Word of God. Imagine yourself as one of those early followers listening attentively to the words of your teacher.

Pause from your work in this book of finding more authentic ways to carry on your part of the holy conversation. Take a few moments to journal in response to these questions:

- What does the *listening* part of your prayer life sound like?

- Look like?

- At what level do you receive or perceive instructions for incarnating, closing the gap between what is and what can be?

- Does prayer provide you directions about daily activites?

- When you pray do you sense guidance about larger scale issues, such as your life's purpose?

Use your journal to record your contemplation.

INCARNATION IS RELATIONAL

Incarnation is loaded with baggage for some. Heavy baggage. It raises ideas like

- dogma

- indoctrination

- creeds

- sin

- justification

- confessional faith

While some of us like pondering these things, many of us don't. We just want to know what it means for us now in our lives. So, in the same way that unpacking the Lord's Prayer helped us pray it (and other prayers) more authentically, a little unpacking of incarnation may help us see why it matters to us in the context of prayer.

Quaker writer Rufus Jones ties the incarnation to the kingdom of God in a way that makes Jesus' life on earth a key to understanding what it is that we are called to do—including what we're to do in prayer. Jones identifies the early Christians understanding of themselves and their message as,

> on its highest level a new revelation of God, and it was on the human plane an equally new revelation of man's potential nature....

> The fact that God can be revealed in a personal life carries momentous implications. It means that the divine and the human are not so far sundered as had been persistently supposed.... This revealing union of the divine and the human in a life of love and service and self-giving is the clue to another central idea which belongs to the

heart of Christianity—namely the way of life with Christ called "the kingdom of God."

Unpacked simply, the incarnation is the most redemptive act ever known. It joins God and humanity in restored relationship. It's one thing to "hear" Jesus' parables and words on God's love. But we see incarnation fully when he weeps at Lazarus's death. He tells his followers (and us) that we matter to God so much that the very hairs on their heads are numbered, but we see the truth of that care when he weeps in grief.

As we thought about the incarnation, one thing in particular became apparent. The incarnation shows that God is relational. This means, that when we shift attention to God through prayer, we reach toward our conversation partner. God makes spiritual reality vibrant and real—from the beginning and with ongoing creative interaction. The act of prayer is like checking one's compass for magnetic north. Prayer reorients us to spiritual reality, the relationship we have with our Creator and eternal conversation partner.

Equally important to our lives today, the incarnation calls us into a way of life with Christ that is manifest in the ongoing conversation of prayer. We are his disciples in this day. Again, Jesus may say that we are his body. We hear that. But we *see* the way that we are to be his body when he sends his disciples out to proclaim the kingdom. We also see it when we are called to authentic prayer—as the people of God.

For Brent, one of the most powerful examples of the body of Christ at prayer occurred when he was a young teen.

> *When I was thirteen, my dad was almost killed in an industrial accident. The doctors held out little hope. The call went out for the members of our church to start a prayer vigil. For a number of days—until they determined that Dad, while still critical, was going to make it—people went to the church and prayed around the clock. From dawn's early light to the darkest hours of night, someone was on his knees or sitting in a pew praying for my dad and our family. Even though I only knew it was happening and wasn't at the church, it's an image that is engraved in my soul. The people of God doing what they could as Christ's body: praying.*

When we consider the multiple ways that incarnation is manifested, we find ourselves taking steps toward our own incarnation as members of the body. We're not perfect. We're not always saintly. The people of Brent's childhood church weren't either. They were broken, flawed, hopeful, believing, caring people who prayed, individually and together.

We, like they, begin to live as citizens in the kingdom when we pray. We practice personal presence. We work to cultivate our awareness of God's presence. We gather together in bodies and small groups, bringing our individual bodies and all the senses we come with to discern the sights, sounds, smells and verbs of God. We do that so we can track God's presence with us and respond to it. Living incarnationally is a life of prayer.

GOD IS RELATIONAL

Many Christians refer to the Trinity in their prayers and liturgies. *Trinity* is a sort of spiritual shorthand to speak of the natures of the one God that have been known in human history in different forms. There is a famous Eastern Orthodox icon that shows the three around a table together. It is a holy Trinity icon, believed to be created by Russian painter Andrei Rublev in the fifteenth century. It's his most famous work.

Holy Trinity icon by Andrei Rublev

In the icon, the gazes and hand positions of the three represent the relation of Christ to Abba to the Holy

Spirit. To this understanding of trinitarian relationship within God we can add the relationship of humanity to each of those aspects or faces of God. God is relational, inwardly and outwardly. The incarnation and the descent of the Holy Spirit are among the proofs of God's ongoing relationship with us.

When we pray, we shift to an awareness of earth as a spiritual place. This is an understanding that life is entirely, or at least simultaneously, a spiritual reality that overlaps the world as it appears to the usually distracted human mind. *God is present. Am I?*

EXERCISE 26—AN INCARNATIONAL PRAYER

Consider the icon image in the previous section. Notice your response to the idea of the three persons of the Trinity sitting around a table together. Heaven only knows what goes on beyond our knowing. Notice how your mind responds to the idea.

In your journal, write a prayer that contains any questions you have about incarnation—either the coming of the Word as Jesus or the coming together of the body of the faithful to witness to their shared glimpses of God's Way for the world. Or both.

Knowing that God is deeply relational, within the mystery of the Trinity and outwardly with humanity, open yourself to admissions of your desires for relationship, and practice again the prayer of listening.

You might want to thank God for the mystery of incarnational relationship. You might want to pray for courage to be faithful in spite of whatever you're struggling with. Living into incarnational prayer is like the conversation between Jesus and the child's father in Mark 9:23-24. The disciples had tried to drive a spirit out of a child and failed. The father begged Jesus to help, if he could. "If I can?" said Jesus. "Everything is possible for one who believes. Immediately the boy's father exclaimed, 'I do believe; help me overcome my unbelief!'" Are there aspects related to incarnation, or to prayer, about which you would say, "I believe; heal my unbelief?"

LIFE PRAYER

Quakers are big on peace. That may be the one thing many people know about us. That and oatmeal. (In reality, oatmeal has nothing to do with Quakers.) We refer to our stance as "the Peace Testimony." While it's the best known, it is not the only "testimony" we have. Friends have a series of corporate witnesses that marry theology with life, which we call the "testimonies." They include such things as

- community

- equality

- integrity

- peace

- simplicity

- stewardship

We have a saying about these testimonies: "Let your life speak." It means that as followers of Jesus, we let our lives speak—in words, if necessary—as a witness to the power of the gospel.

What we call life prayer is a way of letting your life speak with prayer. Life prayer is responding with your life to what you perceive and believe about God, humanity and the relationship between the two. Life prayer takes prayer out of the closet, the church, the privacy of your mind, and into visible witness—testimony—spoken by your life. Those who come close enough to witness your life should be able to "hear" your testimonies by observing your life. Through hearing your testimonies, they may catch a glimpse of God and the kingdom to which you are responding.

Life prayer is a lifestyle choice, in the same way that being vegetarian or going to the gym every day is. Of course, because of its spiritual dynamic, it affects us even more profoundly than most other lifestyle choices do. We have found life prayer is a habituation, a basic orientation in our lives. While we are not perfect at it, any more than we are at working out, we have seen in our lives that it is achieved by practice. We need to cultivate routine pauses to consider, respond to, and be aware of our lenses and our baggage. When we do so, nothing prevents us from seeing and responding to the glimpse of the Holy.

The focus of life prayer is to deepen the holy conversation. If your life and actions touch another specifically or make imperceivable but effective ripples that aid in bridging the gap between God's Way and the present way, then you are incarnating.

EXERCISE 27—LIFE PRAYER

Take a moment to call to mind a subject that you have been meaning to carry into prayer. Pick the first subject that arises. As soon as you have the subject in mind, begin to pray aloud spontaneously. Listen to your words. Notice the length and pacing of your prayer. Pay attention to how you feel. Pray until you are empty of prayer, at least on this subject.

Allow yourself a break for tea, a walk around the house or to connect briefly with someone in person or by phone, or with a pet.

Now return to prayer. This time use a pencil and paper to craft a prayer on the same subject as your spontaneous prayer. It doesn't have to be long, but let it be as complete as the first prayer on the same topic. Pray it aloud. Again, listen to your words. Notice the length and pacing. Is it shorter or longer? Faster or slower? Does it make you feel different than your spontaneous prayer did?

Notice if the subject that came to mind initially seemed more suited to spontaneous spoken prayer or the crafted/written prayer. If so, what makes it more suitable for one form than the other?

If you allow additional subjects to come to mind after completing the exercise, pay attention to whether your prayer profile (what you pray about most often) lends itself to one or another kind of prayer. Do you have a bias in favor of or against one or the other forms of prayer? If you have a bias, what is it? What do you think are the roots of that bias? Is there any action that you need to take in regard to your bias?

INCARNATION, LANGUAGE AND PUBLIC PRAYER

"So, will you say the prayer?" That's what some old friends he was having dinner with asked Brent, their former pastor, recently. It's not an unusual occurrence for either Brent or Jennie. As retreat leaders and public ministers, we're often asked to give public prayers. That may be true for you too.

Like us, even if you are comfortable with personal prayer and use different styles of prayer for different topics and occasions, you may still find yourself at a pause when you are asked to offer public prayers that aren't historical or liturgical ones. Besides Brent's fear of public prayer brought on by the childhood trauma of his cousin's spiritual-sounding prayers, there is a very good reason for this. Seeking and finding the verbs of God is intense and personal work. And that's for our private prayers. The process may also be undertaken in a faith community, but this is also intense and takes time. As individuals, doing this work we become sensitized to this process and to the centrality of the prayer relationship. Even if we're used to praying in public, we find ourselves increasingly sensitive about choosing these words for others. *What if our imagery is too far out? What if my prayer words reveal that I do not share the theology of those with whom I am praying?* These fears compound if you're shy about speaking in public. This fear is a particular kind of fear—and it's not entirely bad. It keeps us aware and thoughtful.

Being aware of the theological lenses you wear and the accompanying assumptions and inherited notions of God you carry is part of the process you have experienced in looking at prayer. It's resulted in your giving depth and attention to the most important conversation of your life. But not everyone you encounter in public prayer spaces has done this work. And not everyone who has done this work has God language that matches yours. That's why it is important for us to remember that public prayer is primarily still a conversation with the Holy. The only difference is that if you are praying publicly, you have invited others to overhear your part of the holy conversation.

Depending on your language, you may be "the voice" in prayer. Or you may be praying as the spokesperson for a gathered group. Your prayer may include "I ask," or in the final phrase, you may say, "In the name of Jesus, I pray." You may bring the invitation to prayer to include others by asking for joys and concerns to incorporate in your shared spontaneous prayer, or you may simply say, "Please join your hearts with mine in prayer." Whatever language you use, you are sharing your understanding of God with those who hear your prayer. Whether or not you mention those three theological questions about what is implied about God, humanity, and the relationship between God and humans, hearers will draw conclusions based on what you say.

For centuries, contemplative artists have captured stories from Scripture in paintings, sculptures and poems. The arts, though, no matter how beautiful and compelling their creation, cannot capture the image of God. They only reflect an *afterimage.* This afterimage is evidence of a human's noticing of God. Searching for such evidence in art is another kind of grace-spotting. In the case of contemplative art and personal prayer, both artists and artful pray-ers respond with words, paints and other media to the holy sensations that remain after a holy encounter.

In the arts, what is created and shared often sufficiently captures the echo of divine presence in ways that people viewing the artist's response to God also feel God. There is a nearly indescribable, but absolutely perceivable, inner "aha" of recognition in catching the shared glimpse of God. In the same way that this happens through the arts, so too does it happen in the language of shared prayer.

This includes public prayer. In praying authentically in public, we create something that conveys the mystical wonder of the reality of God sufficiently so that others hearing the prayer are invited into that same awe of God. The response of the pray-er to God is the prayer she speaks. By seeing the response of the pray-er, the observer begins to perceive the thing responded to, perhaps in a new light.

Life prayer is about *your* incarnation and holy conversation with God. This includes public prayer. You might have an opportunity to share this conversation publicly

- in leadership roles in communities

- when praying with someone as a gesture of companionship

- when your perspective on a situation allows you to see God and the person who needs prayer in a way that the person cannot themselves see

Public prayer comes out of your life prayer. The words suit the context, but they also reflect your understandings of God and humanity and the relationship between them. This "between the lines" message is powerful and can change the hearts of hearers.

EXERCISE 28—WORD OF GOD AND OUR WORDS

Incarnation is a central concept of Christian faith. The coming of Jesus changed everything. In faith communities all over the world, the rippling effects of newcomers connecting with Jesus are still changing everything. One by one, these hearts step into relationship with the mystery of the Word of God, the expression of God's love entered into the world in a human life.

Take a moment to reread some of the prayers you have written in previous exercises. Also review the lists about the nature of God and the list and prayers related to things that seem absolutely impossible reflections of God. It's time to make a new list. You may have heard of "the elevator speech." Entrepreneurs and sales people develop their pitch so that if given the opportunity to talk to someone about their passion for ninety seconds on an elevator, they have it on the tip of their tongue. What prayer is on the tip of your tongue?

Make a list of three to five things you would absolutely want a person hearing your public prayer to know about God and God's relationship with humanity. Think in brief phrases. How would you convey those most important aspects of your faith understanding if your "elevator speech" were public prayer?

Jennie's list (on a given day, prone to vary):

- God loves

- God knows us

- God has plans and intentions for the world

- God wants to collaborate with us

So, if asked to offer a spontaneous public prayer before a meal, Jennie might offer:

Loving God,

> Thank you for this time together, and for the food and fellowship that we are to enjoy. There are surely joys and concerns that have not been lifted up in the group, but you know them already. In all true leadings, help us to have willing hearts and wisdom to discern our way. Help us to use this nourishment of food and companionship to strengthen us for the work to be done.

In the name of Jesus, I pray...

Public prayer is a witness, and can be a valuable tool for inviting others into awe. We must remember that beyond any of our words that may be overheard, seeds planted by God crack open in a person and create a longing for communication with God the Creator. When we engage in prayers that will be overheard by others, we provide a glimpse into what we have come to know about God. Public prayer is a testimony to the holy conversation and an invitation for others to join it. Your willingness to be seen using authentic language and expressing yourself vulnerably may be imperfect, but it is also inspired, and inspiring.

PRAYING IN THE BODY

"Do you know what your body's saying when you sit like that?" That's what a workshop leader asked Brent once.

> *"It means I like to sit this way?" I answered. I was sitting slumped in the chair, arms folded and my eyes closed. What it meant to me was that I was comfortable and concentrating. I hear better with my eyes closed. I focus on the words being said.*
>
> *To her, though, based on her training in body language, my body was communicating that I was disengaged and unreceptive.*
>
> *I sat up straight, unfolded my arms and kept my eyes open for the next two days!*

So what does this have to do with using our experiences of God and new language to pray? For one, it serves as a reminder that we are not just minds, mouths and souls. We are bodies too. It also reminds us that our bodies have their own language—a language that we can bring to prayer in fresh ways.

In much of this book we've dealt with the prayer of the lips—the words. But we humans are more than lips! One of the things we've been learning over the years is how to connect our bodies to our spirituality. Since this book is about learning a new language, we encourage you to think about body language. That means using your whole self in prayer.

> # A Breath Prayer
>
> Jesus heal me (on intake of breath), Make me whole (on exhalation).
>
> **Catharine Phillips**

We bring our whole selves to God in prayer when we do so incarnationally. For too long Christians in America have made our faith disembodied. We are in some ways modern-day gnostics. We are content to live our lives in the heart/head/spirit's knowledge of God while ignoring (at best) or distrusting (at worst) our bodies. When Jesus took himself off alone to pray, however, he did not leave his body behind. He took it with him. As should we.

Another way prayer becomes incarnational is when we pay attention to our body's language. The concept "Let your life speak" is meant to be an admonition to let your daily actions reflect godliness as much as your words, but it can also be understood in another way: What is your life/body saying to you?

Our bodies are carriers of spiritual wisdom—something we often forget. They speak to us all the time. What is your body saying to you in its unique language? Does it ache with pain from overwork? Is it at peace and calm? Does your stomach gurgle and let you know it's time to eat?

While we can make too much of this body language, we can also make too little. Indeed, the noise and sensations of our body can be used as reminders that Jesus also experienced these things. They can remind us of the needs of the rest of the mystical body that is Christ incarnate on this earth. Thus our body language can draw us closer to Jesus the God-man who walked across this earth experiencing hunger and the need for a good bath *and* closer to God's children around this earth. Our brothers and sisters in faith are wearing bodies like we do.

BODY LANGUAGE

As you think about what it means to pray incarnationally, consider what Ben Campbell Johnson says:

> Incarnational prayer may begin with the prayer of the lips (words), but it also includes the eyes (vision and images), the mind (ideas and thought), the heart (feelings and emotions), the hands (service), the feet (obedience) and the ear (listening).

Ponder Johnson's words. How would you include your eyes in incarnational prayer? Might it be through visualizing Jesus visiting a lonely friend for whom you've been praying? How would this be different from just saying words requesting that God ease your friend's loneliness? Might praying with your feet actually mean becoming Jesus in the sense that you would go visit this friend? That you would become the incarnation, bringing good news of glad tidings to this one that you love?

Take a few moments and answer the question How can you imagine using the following in prayer?

- your eyes

- your mouth

- your ears

- your skin

- your hands

- your feet

- your nose

Praying incarnationally means that we ourselves become the prayer—body, mind and soul. In doing so, we both experience and participate in the incarnation. We become molded into the likeness of Christ and live into being his body in this world. And it makes a world of difference. That's because the message of the incarnation is love.

Jesus' idea is irresistible and irreversible. Even unbelievers must live within it. For love doesn't stand alone, nor can it, *but trails like a blazing comet, bringing with it other shining goods—forgiveness, kindness, tolerance, fairness, companionship and friendship—all bound to the love at the heart of Jesus' message.*

Incarnational prayer helps us to fully incarnate this love in and to the world. As we walk closer to the heart of God, we become lights in an often dark world, bringing such shining goods as love, joy, peace, forbearance, kindness, goodness, faithfulness, gentleness and self-control. The power of incarnational prayer unfolds into a life of faithful response to the holy conversation.

8

Beyond Words

OTHER WAYS OF COMMUNICATING—OR NOT

Therefore I will not keep silent;
I will speak out in the anguish of my spirit,
I will complain in the bitterness of my soul.

JOB 7:11

Not today. Maybe tomorrow." That's what Brent's four-year-old grandson Ayden says when he doesn't want to do something. He learned it from his parents, who used it as an answer to things such as "Can we get ice cream today?" or "Can we go visit Gee-Gee?" It has backfired, obviously. Now he uses it on them.

Sometimes we feel that way about prayer. We don't feel like doing it. "Not today. Maybe tomorrow." Sometimes it could be because the words just won't come. Or we don't want them to come. Especially words from our most authentic selves. There are times when we just can't drag the words forth. A sad silence shrouds our souls. Our thoughts whirl but our tongues won't move. So we use a different language from engagement—the language of inaction.

There is no way we could write authentically about prayer without spending some time looking at the uncomfortable realities of prayer. While we earnestly believe that deepening our prayer lives leads us to increased authenticity in our relationship with God, we also know that our life of prayer isn't always pleasant, encouraging or consistent. We attempt to press on, believing that regardless of the situation, all prayer is communication with God. Even the less comfortable experiences of prayer communicate something to us, whether in words or in some other form of language.

RESISTANCE

Like Ayden, we exercise our wills all the time—including negatively. In the same way it is possible to resist temptations and perils by exercising our will, it is also possible to resist spiritual growth by exercising our will. Not to pick on you, but if you have been skipping exercises in this book, you may be resisting. We're not shaking our fingers and murmuring "tsk tsk." We're just acknowledging that skipping exercises could be a form of resistance. Bless your hearts (that's a phrase in the Midwest that softens any criticism).

The reason we bring it up is that we're inviting you to consider what kinds of resistance you engage in. We know we have resistances, especially related to prayer and our relationship with the Holy.

We offer two types of resistance to consider. The first is charged resistance. Charged resistance is when the refusal to do or consider something takes you away from the experience of inner freedom. When we say inner freedom, we mean a release from negatives such as compulsive behaviors, denial, blaming others or circumstances, and living into positives like feelings of wholeness and connection with God. Charged resistance is also often dispassionate. You just don't care that you just don't care.

Jennie encountered charged resistance in herself recently when slacking off on her daily spiritual practice routine, which includes yoga, prayer and writing. At first, she skipped a day here and there. Then it quickly turned into a month of not doing. She told herself and her husband that she was busy, tired, not feeling well. When she finally got back to a single day of practice, she felt sadness, uncertainty and grief about something from the past, all at the same time. Some part of her knew these things were beneath the surface. She avoided feeling and dealing with these uncomfortable emotions by eschewing spiritual practice altogether.

The second kind of resistance is called uncharged resistance. Uncharged resistance may be distraction, exhaustion, the need to prioritize, or something else legitimate. In the case of uncharged resistance, the decision to resist by not doing something has no further echo or ripple in our lives or minds. It is not a "who cares" kind of looking away in fear, anger or frustration. Rather it is a state of being in which the decisions you make and actions you take are chosen with a clarity of mind and heart that leaves you peaceful.

For Brent, uncharged resistance often appears when he feels led to say no to something he's been asked to do. Especially when it's something worthy or good. As part of practicing self-care (a hard lesson for him to learn!), he's learned not to overcommit himself. He feels internal resistance when he's on the verge of overcommitting. As such, he's said no to opportunities he would have liked to participate in and the chance to be with people he likes to spend time with. Once he's said no to something from the standpoint of self-care, though, he lets it go. He feels contentment with that decision and rarely thinks of it again.

Procrastination—"Oh, I'll just do it later"—can be either charged or uncharged. Deciding to go to the movies instead of mowing the lawn may come with no further effect. Especially if you're an adult and it's your lawn. The next morning you wake up and mow. The resistance from the previous day is forgotten and all is well until the grass grows back. If, however, you're the teenager and your parents told you to mow the lawn, then the resistance may be charged.

The next exercise will help you examine your resistance to praying—where it's coming from and how to consciously work on any blocks between you and increased intimacy with God. Even if—or especially if—that intimacy feels fearful.

> ### "Suscipe (Receive)"
>
> Take, Lord, and receive all my liberty,
>
> my memory, my understanding
>
> and my entire will,
>
> All I have and call my own.
>
> You have given all to me.
>
> To you, Lord, I return it.
>
> Everything is yours; do with it what you will.
>
> Give me only your love and your grace.
>
> That is enough for me.
>
> **St. Ignatius of Loyola (1491–1556)**

EXERCISE 29—MY RESISTANCE

One way to determine if the resistance you are experiencing is charged or uncharged is to look behind the curtains of your mind and heart to see the real reasons you are resisting. That can be scary. You might not want to get into the real reasons you resist. Perhaps it feels safer emotionally and spiritually to resist. Perhaps it feels that not to resist is a sort of surrender of your free will and independence. Think again about the three questions.

- What does my resistance say about what I think about God's nature?

- What does my resistance say about what I think about human nature or humanity?

- What does my resistance say about what I think about the relationship between God and me as a human being?

If you hear your answers expressing fear or blame or anger, consider them an invitation to tap into your feelings. Acknowledge your feelings in all their rawness. Then look at your resistance in this new light.

If you feel a vague unwillingness, as Jennie did about her daily practice, it may be a good idea to quit resisting. That way you can see what lies beneath it and decide if it's charged or uncharged. If it's uncharged, you may not need to do anything about your resistance. If it is charged, however, you will want to explore why it is so.

THE BUSINESS OF OBEDIENCE

"Kate 'will not obey'" screamed the headline of a *Daily Mail* edition reporting an update on the marriage plans of Kate Middleton and Prince William. While this may have been shocking news in the United Kingdom, it was not much of a surprise here. It's been decades since most brides have included that word in their wedding vows.

Brent has been officiating weddings since the 1970s and can't recall any that included vows using the word *obey*. *Obey* is an uncomfortable word for many of us—especially in regard to relationships. One reason it's unpopular is that we have so much wealth and freedom in the West that we loathe yielding our will to anyone outside of ourselves. Another reason could be the result of misuse or misunderstandings of what obedience is and isn't. We might resist authentic prayer and anything that could lead us deep into it because we're afraid that we might be called to obedience.

Obedience and change. Obedience could mean change *especially* when it's obedience to something we're pretty sure we won't want to do. One of the ironic things we've discovered about our charged resistance to prayer is that it often is signaling a stage of spiritual unfolding. Many times charged resistance immediately precedes obedience. We're resisting because change is coming! As Harry Emerson Fosdick writes, "Prayer, when it is real, is the innermost way in which anyone who believes in God makes earnest business of his faith."

Making earnest business of faith is about letting God guide our lives. Our scriptural ancestors seemed to recognize their need for guidance and obedience much more easily than we do. Of course, they were not always as obedient as they said they would be. Just look at the examples of the Israelites from the Old Testament or Peter in the New Testament. God sends various judges, kings and prophets to call the Israelites to obedience. And they are obedient for a while. And then they aren't.

Surrender. *Surrender,* like obedience, is a word we don't care for all that much these days. From Brent's family Fantasy Football team to Jennie's ceaseless electronic Scrabble, we want to be or back winners. Winners don't surrender. They fight with all their strength to not give in and instead to prevail. Except in God's kingdom. Darnnit.

We sometimes resist going deeper in prayer because heading toward obedience feels like a surrender of sorts. Indeed, it is surrender. Even if it's surrender that results in increased intimacy with God.

But experience has shown us that when we follow the way of Jesus—when we surrender our wills to the divine will—we actually find ourselves living more fully as ourselves than ever before. That's part of the upside-down, contrary-to-this-world life with God. "For whoever wants to save their life will lose it, but whoever loses their life for me will find it" (Matthew 16:25).

Still ... surrender. Maybe it reminds us of "Surrender Dorothy" written in the sky in *The Wizard of Oz.* Scary. We don't want to. So we resist.

A place we don't want to go. Another thing that makes the pull to obedience hard to follow is that, while we have learned that it is an invitation to go deeper, it can take us to places we are not sure we want to go. Or places we're certain that we *don't* want to go.

For one, acknowledging our resistances to prayer and obedience may lead us into a spiritual desert. Writing about contemplative prayer, Thomas Merton noted:

> This climate in which monastic prayer flowers is that of the desert, where the comfort of man is absent, where the secure routines of man's city offer no support, and where prayer must be sustained by God in the purity of faith.

Yes, we have biblical and other stories of the fruitful experiences of being spiritual in the desert. But those were about saints. Not us. The notion of retaining a pure faith and a focused belief in the midst of our resistance and God's absence seems impossible. It's hard enough in Eden (just look at Eve and Adam) when one is standing in the middle of the desert.

Rejection. We may be afraid that if we admit that common emotions of fear, blame and anger are inescapable aspects of our humanity, we are unlovable and unloved. This is especially true if the reason for our resistance has any relational context with humans or God. We hate being abandoned by friends and lovers. It's horrible. And so we want to avoid feeling desolation and abandonment by God that we fear will come should we dare to overcome our resistances and reveal ourselves wholly to the Holy.

Call screening. Jennie describes a small group of longtime, dear friends as "the people I would call at 3a.m." This is her shorthand for those intimate companions whose love and forgiveness for the timing of and reason for the call is something she can count on if she ever needs to make a 3a.m. call. She knows they'll pick up.

Sometimes, because of all our human flaws, we wonder if God is a 3a.m. friend. Might, just might God be screening the calls? "Oh, it's Brent—I think I'll let this go to voicemail. He calls all the time, never listens anyhow, so he can wait till a more convenient time." On the face of it, we know that's absurd. Theologically, it's untenable. At least for everyone else—God hears their calls. But ours?

This is a good place to remember that even though we attribute characteristics to God that are within our human capacity for knowing (emotions, thoughts, decisions) and also characteristics that we do not possess (constancy, transcendency, omnipotence), God is more. More than we can imagine, and certainly more than we can know in any absolute way. This does not decrease the primal urge we have for connection with our Creator. It does not decrease the rational urge we have for making meaning either. It is a reminder to pause at the edge of certainty. That's especially true when our certainty edges close to our thinking that we know everything we need to know about the character and nature of God. We are on the trail of the Holy with our paying attention to our encounters and the encounters of our spiritual ancestors, but we must remember it is a search that will not yield full knowledge.

If God were screening our calls, our prayers, then we would have to wrestle with what that means about the nature of God and our relationship with God. It would definitely correct any residual childish notions we carry of God as a vending machine into which we can drop our prayer nickels and push a button for results.

God is not a vending machine. Nor is God an old friend whom we can know as well as we know ourselves. We cannot know God's response to our 3a.m. prayers. But we need to make the call anyway. It will be picked up.

It is our nature to reach toward the Holy. Doing so in the shadow of the fear of not being answered is a sign of our spiritual maturity and faithful action. Daring to do that takes us one step further along the pilgrim way of real conversation.

EXERCISE 30—RESISTING THE CALL

When it comes to calling on God, one reason for resistance comes from some of the things you may have written down earlier—the words you were uncomfortable using about God's nature or feared might be true. Not one of us is going to call if we're afraid that nobody's home. Or worse, that someone is home and they are screening calls. Especially when that someone is God.

Return to that list of words you made that you feared might be true about God. Review it. Pick two or three words that are most charged for you. Then complete the following sentences for each word on your shortened list. Take your time. This exercise is a real stretch.

- If God is _____, then I can/could never _____.

- If God is _____, then I have been wrong about _____.

- If God is_____, that changes everything. I don't know what I would believe about _____.

Jennie's example:

> If God is a judge and a hater, then I can never let myself be seen as I truly am.

> If God is a judge and hater, then I have been wrong about the Christian call to radical forgiveness and compassion.

> If God is a judge and a hater, that changes everything. I don't know what I would believe about the kingdom and my relationship to it.

> O Lord, baptize our hearts into a sense of the conditions and needs of all people.
>
> **George Fox (1624–1691)**

After you have made your list and filled in the blanks, read your sentences aloud. Notice if the second part of each sentence is a fear or concern that leads you to resistance in prayer even though you don't believe the characteristics of God match the first part of the sentence. In doing this exercise, we found that we carry our fears and doubts with us, and they may surface in times of resistance.

NIGHTMARES

SyFy's annual *Twilight Zone* marathon is one of Brent's favorite guilty pleasures. Its familiar theme music and stories of things that are not what they seem still intrigue him after more than fifty years. Most of the stories feature some sort of existential crisis. The best part is that these crises are fictional and happening to someone else—not us!

Many Christians have a life experience akin to a *Twilight Zone* one, and it can be a source of resistance. St. John of the Cross, a Spanish saint who lived in the mid-to-late 1500s, famously called this experience the dark night of the soul. As he described it, the dark night is the experience of Christians seeking for God and feeling both distant from the world *and* from communion with God. Rod Serling had nothing on St. John of the Cross.

The dark night of the soul operates on two levels. One is the material world of the body. The second is the inner world of the spirit. Contemporary writer and psychiatrist Gerald May writes: "In life, the process is often marked by a feeling of emptiness and lack of energy for the old ways of living. Similarly, one often experiences a growing dryness in the old ways of praying and an absence of consolation and lack of energy for meditation."

Fosdick, whom we mentioned earlier, brings prayer into the discussion of the dark night when he says, "True prayer is fulfilling the conditions of our relationship with this Spiritual World." He explains that even as the physical world is around our bodies "this spiritual world" is in and around our spirits. We are more than physical beings. Yes, intellectually we know that. We often forget it, though, even in our lives as followers of Jesus. That's why we need to own that our spirit dwells in and is affected by a world of spirit. This spiritual world is the one we affect in prayer.

It is also the world we resist entering when we're in the dark night of the soul. Often times we just don't have the energy, beset as we are with dryness or desolation or despair or depression. There are other words that we could use. Many others. Each of them has a different flavor or feeling. Some—like *abandonment*—emphasize emotional terror. Others, such as *emptiness,* focus on a level of perception. Those feelings are hard to break through.

Once again, we've found that resistance—in this case in the midst of the dark night of the soul—can be a precursor to growth. May says the dark night is the experience one has on the way toward inner freedom. It's a freedom we experience as we move closer toward ease in the holy conversation:

> As I have said, the dark night of the soul is an ongoing transition from compulsively trying to control one's life toward a trusting freedom and openness to God and the real situations of life. It is the same in prayer, where the effort and forceful focusing of meditation are gradually eased, and the more willing receptivity of contemplation grows.

May's "lack of energy for meditation" is exactly what Jennie says was happening in her example of charged resistance. At the time, she would have said her resistance was not charged at all. She would have said that she just lacked energy to continue her daily practices. Once she restarted them, she felt unambiguously that God, as physician to her soul, had called her back to them. God helped her acknowledge and eventually release feelings she had been suppressing and avoiding. The resistance itself, expressed as her lack of energy to pray, write and do yoga, formed into a personal story with echoes of the parable of the prodigal son. She went off to a far land, felt desolate and returned to a loving, embracing home.

We need to realize that the feelings we might be tempted to analyze as mental or psychological struggles are actually the pains of being birthed into a life of inward freedom and more authentic prayer. This was certainly the case for Jennie.

EXERCISE 31—GROWING PAINS

Take a moment to do a quick written inventory of the discomforts and discontents of your life. It may be helpful to consider the larger categories of your life one by one:

- work/career
- family
- friendships
- recreation/hobbies
- faith community
- other categories of importance

Be honest in your assessments.

Take another spin through your list of discomforts and note any resistances you experience in those areas. For example, if work is challenging, acknowledge the tasks you have delayed. Or the colleague you avoid.

Try to use "I" statements to name how you respond to your discomforts with resistance.

Now review your inventory category by category. Consider whether these may be birth pains of a new way of being in relationship to the Holy. Where are there possible invitations to depth seeded in your discomforts?

Like Jennie's example of returning to daily spiritual practice melting her resistance, are there actions you could take that oppose your resisting actions? Might they, if you tried them, create shifts in your perspective (from discomfort to deepening) or in your actions?

PRAY ANYWAY

One of the hardest lessons we've learned is that when we are tempted to stop praying, we need to press on. Yes, prayer is dangerous business. When we find ourselves staring into the face of holy obedience, we may blink. We may not feel ready to be changed by the divine encounter. We imagine that the safest thing we can do is avert our eyes and our hearts from more provoking prayer conversations.

We have spoken in earlier chapters about how the images of God as mother or mother hen have deep roots in the Christian tradition. Now imagine a child (or a chick) denying the nurture of the one who birthed him because he did not have a full understanding of how things worked. That's a powerful image of resistance. Perhaps we act like that in times of deep prayer. Our level of willingness to see and be seen increases or decreases in proportion to our feeling of vulnerability, whether physical, mental, emotional or spiritual.

Certainly that is true for the psalmists who express anger, fear or frustration, and speak emphatically. We can imagine the psalmists speaking personally to God, conveying personal expectations and hopes to a God whom they understand has a personal connection to them. They don't understand everything else about how God operates. But they understand the relationship between God and humankind enough to trust.

Relationship is key. Relationship cannot be accomplished (at a human level) with the entire world. When we have a relationship with a person it's with *a* person. Singular. When it is with one person it becomes—obviously—personal. So too with God. Prayer is a way of making it personal and a relationship—if, that is, we move from remote to personal references of God. From "O God in heaven above" to "Abba" or "Mother Hen."

When we move to the personal, prayer begins. Life-changing prayer. Casting-doubt-aside prayer. Dropping third person ways of speaking about God—such as *he, she, it* or *God* and moving to *you* or *thou*—moves us from speaking *about* God to speaking *with* God. We are no longer sitting across a metaphorical room making commentary about that distant God over there; we are sitting with God in conversation. That conversation is prayer.

So don't stop praying. Don't stop even if it doesn't make sense. Even if it makes you uncomfortable. Even if you start to wonder if your prayer calls are being screened. Keep going.

Persistent prayer is not stubbornness, even though it may feel like it. We may think that we should pray only when we feel like it. We might think that prayer should spring spontaneously from our souls or pop into our minds as needed. This happens sometimes. But moving deeply into prayer is more like taking a sea voyage in a small boat. We launch out from the safe shore with a hungering heart that yearns to know God more deeply and intimately. Our destination is the face of a loving God. We sail over an ocean that is sometimes smooth with spiritual wind filling our sails and souls. Other times we find ourselves becalmed. We sit and wait for a breeze. In a dark night.

Or we are in danger of being swamped by doubt. The waves peak and fall, we are tossed and directionless. We hold on for dear life. We cry out, like the disciples rocking on the Sea of Galilee, "Teacher, don't you care if we drown?" (Mark 4:38). Then we lift the oars of prayer and begin to row. Even when it seems helpless. Eventually we break through and find ourselves propelled by fresh winds of the spirit.

Persistent prayer is a chance for God to break through, for Jesus to say "Quiet! Be still!" (Mark 4:39) to the waves and winds in our lives. The departure pier of prayer is a hungering heart—a life that yearns to know God more intimately.

Henri Nouwen lifts up the value of prayer, regardless of the outcome. Sticking to it is a source of safety.

> Prayer heals. Not just the answer to prayer. When we give up our competition with God and offer God every part of our heart, holding back nothing at all, we come to know God's love for us and discover how safe we are in his embrace. Once we know again that God has not rejected us, but keeps us close to his heart, we can find again the joy of living, even though God might guide our life in a different direction from our desires.

Resistance, absence, discomfort may all exist within your relationship of prayer. See them as invitations to come closer, deeper, to be less guarded in your end of the conversation.

GET OUTTA YER HEAD

When we're stuck, it helps to get out of our heads. One of the ways to do that is by using our bodies to express resistance—or our desire to break through it.

Think about it. Our bodies often indicate our mood or what we're feeling. They are signboards for what we feel in hearts and are thinking in our minds. We've had sweaty palms when we've been faced with an important task or are looking at a new possible mate. We shake our fists at the driver in the car that just cut us off; no words needed there. We close our eyes and relax our entire selves when we hear a beautiful piece of music that overwhelms us.

Do we have that many physical responses to prayer? Not likely. Generally, we find a prayer posture and stick to it. A common one is eyes closed, head bowed, hands folded in imitation of Albrecht Dürer's famous drawing *Study of the Hands of an Apostle.* While an imitation of an apostle could be good at lots of levels, to assume only that one posture of prayer could be shortchanging ourselves, especially in relation to incarnational prayer.

Scripture is filled with prayer postures.

- *Standing:* "Then Solomon stood before the altar of the Lord in front of the whole assembly of Israel, spread out his hands toward heaven" (1 Kings 8:22).

- *Eyes toward heaven:* "After Jesus said this, he looked toward heaven and prayed" (John 17:1).

- *Prostrate:* "And Joshua fell on his face to the earth and worshiped" (Joshua 5:14 NRSV).

- *Placing your head between your knees:* "Elijah climbed to the top of Carmel, bent down to the ground and put his face between his knees" (1 Kings 18:42).

- *Hands raised:* "Therefore I want the men everywhere to pray, lifting up holy hands" (1 Timothy 2:8).

- *Bowing:* "With what shall I come before the Lord and bow down before the exalted God?" (Micah 6:6).

- *Sitting:* "Then King David went in and sat before the Lord" (2 Samuel 7:18).

- *Kneeling:* "Let us kneel before the Lord our Maker" (Psalm 95:6).

The Bible doesn't just have postures associated with prayer either. Luke 18 gives us the example of the tax collector who "would not even look up to heaven, but beat his breast and said, 'God, have mercy on me, a sinner!'" (Luke 18:13).

Think of your usual prayer posture or physical actions. Why did you choose them? Why do they work for you? How do they keep you from new experiences of prayer?

Now consider a prayer you pray often. At the same time, think about your usual prayer posture. Do the prayer and your posture match? Do the meditations of your heart and the words of your mouth fit with the position of your body? If not, what posture would work better? You might even consider different postures for different parts of your prayer.

EXERCISE 32—GET INTO YOUR BODY

What is your response to the suggestion of body prayer? If you are feeling resistance, can you tell if it is charged or uncharged resistance? Are there any invitations, in the guise of resistance or as other discomforts, that may be inviting you to a deeper place?

Let's use the Lord's Prayer as an example of how that might work. Pick a posture or action that would fit each phrase and write down some suggestions as shown in the sample chart.

Think about how you might involve your body in prayer—to bring your whole self to the holy conversation.

Prayer Postures

Prayer	Posture or Action
Our Father,	
who art in heaven,	
hallowed be thy name.	
Thy kingdom come.	
Thy will be done,	
on earth as it is in heaven.	
Give us this day our daily bread.	
And forgive us our trespasses,	

Prayer	Posture or Action
as we forgive those who trespass against us.	
And lead us not into temptation,	
but deliver us from evil. Amen.	

WILLINGNESS

Seeing resistance and accepting it is a first step toward willingness to change. Willingness is mustard-like. From a small seed grows a mighty plant. As we unclench from certainty, we soften the hard lines we have drawn around God; they become permeable. As we allow our images of God to change from negative/unhelpful images to positive/helpful ones, we open up a relationship of prayer that becomes a dynamic, flowing, all-encompassing, inescapable backdrop for our entire lives. The clarity that God is bigger than we can imagine takes us further along our unending search for intimacy. We continue to look for evidence of God's presence because we are convinced that it exists and is worth finding.

> The reason we can hope to find God is that He is here, engaged all the time in finding us. Every gleam of beauty is a pull toward Him. Every pulse of love is a tendril that draws us in His direction. Every verification of truth links the finite mind up into a Foundational Mind that undergirds us. Every deed of good will points toward a consummate

Goodness which fulfills all our tiny adventures in faith. We can find Him because in Him we live and move and have our being.

That is the good news. Both prayer and hope require our full participation. We cannot find God if we invest just a small part of ourselves in prayer. Prayer tends the business and busyness of our lives. We need to be in prayer even as we move through the outward activities of our days. We can learn to live in the deep places of the spirit even in the midst of busyness or chaos. But we can only do that if we're all in—whole-heartedly, whole soully.

Are you willing to have your life permeated by the holy conversation? Are you willing to pray your way toward the simplicity on the far side of complexity, even if the complexity is of your own making?

If so, then pray on. For the way to authentic Holy Conversations is made only by praying. And praying. And praying some more. A pilgrimage of prayer.

9

Gospel Means Good News

AND NEWS IS *NEW,* BY DEFINITION

*I bring you good news that will cause
great joy for all the people.*

LUKE 2:10

Just a month old, Brent's great-granddaughter Evelynne struggled to breathe. Her parents rushed her to the hospital. Brent's wife, Nancy, had already had one grandchild die, almost literally in her arms. Brent and Nancy were beyond frantic and scared. Nancy prayed a desperate, from-the-heart prayer.

> I stood at the dining room windows overlooking the prairie and prayed. I prayed the only words I could....

The sky was filled with clouds. One separated itself and took, incredibly, the shape of a dove. The sun shone through and I was filled with an overwhelming sense of peace. I still didn't know what was going to happen, but I knew I could face whatever came.

God's great love was revealed, though it sounds like a cliché, in this literal parting of the clouds with the sun breaking through. Nancy's epiphany experience reminds us of two important things. First, our God is a revelatory God. And second, this revelation is good news—even when it may not seem so at the time.

Nancy's experience, of course, is not the only instance of God's revelation. Many of us have had our own experiences of God's self-revealing nature. Some of these are seemingly small—the revelation of beauty in the all-but-stereotypical sunset. Others are large and occur in the heart.

God's revelatory nature is not new. It started at the beginning. Literally. "In the beginning God created..." (Genesis 1:1). From the time God created humankind, God he has been busy with the work of revelation. This disclosure continues throughout Scripture—from evening walks in the garden with Adam and Eve to burning bushes with Moses to wrestling matches with Jacob to Gabriel's visit to Mary to the incarnation of Jesus to the gift of the Holy Spirit to us. Jesus continues this revelatory streak through both his life and his words. He often does it through new images—prodigal sons, pearls of great price and lost sheep. Or via concepts that turn the staid, conventional concepts of the divine upside down: peacemakers proclaimed the children of God, the meek given the inheritance of the earth.

Oh, hold them,

> hold them....
>
> Please,
>
> hold them,
>
> hold them up!
>
> **Cat Chapin-Bishop**

Of course, it's not only in Scripture that we read of God's active revelation. There are numerous references in the writings of the saints and mystics of ways God came to them—notably in prayer.

The founder of Quakers, George Fox, wrote about one of his seventeenth-century revelations: "One day, when I had been walking solitarily abroad, and was come home, I was taken up in the love of God, so that I could not but admire the greatness of His love." The more modern mystic St. Thérèse of Lisieux of the nineteenth century had a revelation about God and prayer when she wrote, "How great is the power of Prayer! One could call it a Queen who has at each instant free access to the King and who is able to obtain whatever she asks." That's a powerful personification of prayer—a regent who has the ear of the ruler. And not just the ear but also the heart, so that the king will do what is beseeched. It takes the image of God as king, which is not unfamiliar in the Bible, and changes it to one in which the ruler can be persuaded instead of ruling by fiat or his will only.

While God uses many means of revelation, we have found that prayer is an important channel of that revelation. We who are unbelieving saints bring all our joys and sorrows, longings and lusts, high-mindedness and wickedness to the heart of God. When we open our mouths and hearts and words in prayer, we reveal ourselves to God. As we listen with our hearts and ears God is revealed to us. Prayer shows us the good news of God's commitment to us. It also shows us how God acts in our lives by revealing God's active engagement with us and inviting us into engagement with others. The good news—the news made fresh daily through prayer—is that the life of faith is, at its heart, redemptive. God is redemptive. God is grace and grace-filled.

The experiences of revelation in Scripture, in the prayer lives of the saints and in our own lives of communion show us that God wants to be known in ways that our small human minds and other sensory organs can comprehend. Adam and Eve walked and talked with God in the cool of the day. Moses saw the bush burning but not being consumed. Jacob grappled, sweating. Jesus showed us, through his actions and obedience, a God who loves, heals, comforts, afflicts and much more. Nancy found God's peace in the parting of the clouds.

This next exercise will help you explore how you have experienced God's revelation in your own life.

EXERCISE 33—THE REALITY OF GOD

Take a few minutes now to think of a time when God felt especially real to you. Don't think just about your steadfast belief system. Consider also experiences in your three-dimensional, day-to-day life. As you call that experience to mind, bring as much detail as you can into focus. Look at the situation and see:

- What new image or idea did the experience give you about God?

- What made this experience different from others?

- Why, of all experiences, is this the one that comes to your mind today?

- What made it "real"?

- What did it feel like in your soul?

- What did it feel like in your body?

- Were you being more honest with God than usual? In what ways?

As you think about that experience, also look at whether it came at a time you considered yourself to be praying or not. If you answer no, then you might want to reconsider your definition of prayer. Prayer is nothing more or less than communion and communication with the divine. Any time God breaks through is a time of prayer. And revelation.

PARTICIPATING IN THE MEANING OF REVELATION

One of Brent's favorite stories is William Hoffman's "The Question of Rain." In it, the pastor of a church in a small Virginia town is asked, because of a drought, to hold a "Special Day of Prayer for Rain." The request comes first from a local businessman, whom Hoffman reports, "was generous with his pocket book, but not himself" and who studied the hymns "as if they were corporate reports."

This man, who's concerned about losing business and the resulting layoffs, is just the first to come. Next comes a suggestion from the deacons. Then an officer from the bank appears. Then the women of the church arrive. Wayland, the minister, is uneasy about all these requests. He's not prone to public displays invoking God's favor. "God knows our needs," he says. "He meets them out of His love for us. We don't pray to ask favors as if He's a rich uncle, but to have fellowship with Him, to achieve a feeling that we are close and in His care."

To which one of the church members replies, "Would it hurt to try?"

This is what our souls whisper to us. Would it hurt to try to pray in a new way?

Finally, Wayland, touched by something his wife says, sees that this kind of prayer, when stripped of theology and all the "encrustments" we humans put on it, is merely to plead when troubled. This desire, as one goes to one's loving parent in such circumstances, is human. So, too, it is natural to plead to God when, as his children, we are troubled. So Wayland arranges the service.

You'll have to read the story if you want to know what happens. The point for us is not what the "results" of the prayer service are. Rather, we learn from Wayland's fresh understanding of prayer and his willingness to take his *and* his people's concerns to the God that loves them all.

It's a story that challenges our thinking on prayer by showing that prayer is a way God self-reveals. Prayer demonstrates how God works in our world. Prayer also invites and allows us to participate in the work of God in this world whether we are physically able or bedridden or somewhere in between.

When we pray we are creating. We are renewing the gospel for our times. That's what Wayland did for his people—made the gospel fresh. He helped reveal God's nature to them through their experience of prayer.

Prayer also makes us new. That's wonderful news because none of us want to go through the motions of prayer with no results. The longing that Wayland's people expressed for prayer was not something new or solely theirs. A hunger for authentic prayer that changes people and circumstance is part of the human experience. That hunger is the result of a soul seed sown in us to influence our growth toward God. We find our longing for God growing as our spirits grow. Prayer constantly remakes us, molding us more completely into the image of God.

GOD TALKS BACK

That fact that God talks to us is good news too. Prayer is dialogue. We talk and are talked to. We often think of prayer as us talking to God. As we go deeper and grow our practice of prayer, we learn that prayer is listening at least as much as it is speaking or thinking. It is becoming quiet enough to hear (as 1 Kings) describes it, the "still small voice" (1 Kings 19:12 KJV) that God uses more often than not. When we listen, God is revealed. The good news becomes new!

Oscar Romero, the assassinated archbishop of El Salvador, once wrote:

> This is the beauty of prayer and of Christian life:
> coming to understand that a God
> who converses with humans
> has created them
> and has lifted them up,
> with the capacity of saying
> "I" and "you."
> What would we give to have such power
> as to create a friend to our taste

and with a breath of our own life
to make that friend able to understand us
and be understood by us
and converse intimately—
to know our friend as truly another self?
That is what God has done;
human beings are God's other self.
He has lifted us up
so that he can talk with us and share his joys,
his generosity,
his grandeur.
He is the God who converses with us.

If God is conversing with us then that means, at the very least, half of our prayer time should be spent in listening. Listening is not easy, nor is it the same, for all of us. We begin to pray and we struggle with listening. It doesn't seem natural (at times) and so we try harder. Then we give up. We pray when we think we need to—in cases of emergency or worry—instead of when we really need to, which is all the time. We must realize that when the disciples called to Jesus, begging him to teach them to pray, they were echoing the cry of the human heart throughout all time.

Lord, teach us to pray.
Lord, bring us into your presence.
Lord, show us how to dialogue with you.

That cry implies that we have lessons to be learned. Lessons that come through listening to God's voice.

We have to start where we are. God wants our prayers (speaking and listening) just as they are. Just as we are. As we speak and listen, we are welcomed into God's heart. We are also changed. Our life enlarges as we make more time for God.

We may be surprised at that. *If I take more time—adding listening—to prayer, I will lose more time from my day. And it's busy enough,* we think. Yet, the time we give to prayer comes back to us. No, the minutes are not put back into our twenty-four hours. Nor does the sun stand still (our prayers are probably unlike Joshua's sun-stopping prayer in Joshua 10). Instead, by taking time not just to talk but to listen to God, we find that our rushing slows, our thoughts clear, our priorities reorder themselves along the lines of what God wants. When we listen, we hear the divine, who ordered the universe, giving us instruction that helps us order our lives in ways that bring serenity, space and more energy to our day

Prayer is a means of enlarging our soul's capacity. Of going deeper with God. Of learning more about God's nature and allowing ourselves to be opened to new (or at least new to us) revelations of God's heart. When the desires of God's heart are revealed, we change, we grow, and we become more like the people God wants us to be.

IMAGES OF PRAYER

One of the things that may keep us from praying (or seeing that we are praying) is a list of unpleasant ideas associated with prayer. While we may sing about the "sweet hour" of prayer, you may be like Brent and be thinking, *An hour? My goodness, that would be an eternity!* And prayer can seem that way if our image of it is drudgery. That's why another part of learning a new language for prayer is breaking free from our stereotypes of what prayer is. In the same way that we need to examine our verbs, nouns and adjectives to get to the heart of authentic prayer, so too do we need to examine our prayer habits. Especially if they are pretty rigid or have been around for a long time.

Many of us find ourselves praying at only certain times or occasions. That's true whether we're liturgical and praying the hours or non-liturgical and saying grace before meals or whenever we feel the need or desire to. Or we pray only with certain postures and words.

There is nothing wrong with any of that. However, these prayer habits can rob us of fresh experiences of God's revelation if we expect that communication—that prayer—is only how we tend to experience it. Hence, the need for new ideas about prayer. New ideas about our words, yes, but also what we think about prayers and how and when we pray.

The great spiritual writer Evelyn Underhill gives us a fresh image of prayer when she writes:

> By contemplative prayer, I do not mean any abnormal sort of activity or experience, still less a deliberate and artificial passivity. I just mean the sort of prayer that aims at God in and for Himself and not for any of His gifts whatever, and more and more profoundly rests in Him alone: what St. Paul, that vivid realist, meant by being rooted and grounded. When I read those words, I always think of a forest tree. First of the bright and changeful tuft that shows itself to the world and produces the immense spread of boughs and branches, the succession and abundance of leaves and fruits. Then of the vast unseen system of roots, perhaps greater than the branches in strength and extent, with their tenacious attachments, their fan-like system of delicate filaments and their power of silently absorbing food. On that profound and secret life the whole growth and stability of the tree depend. It is rooted and grounded in a hidden world.

Look at the positive images Underhill offers:

- bright
- abundance
- fruits
- food

- roots
- leaves
- stability
- immense

What imagery most speaks to you? Look into your heart. Pay attention to what bubbles up there.

EXERCISE 34—NEW IMAGES OF PRAYER

What's your image of prayer? Take a few moments to list the words or images that first pop into your mind when you hear the word *prayer*. We'll prime your word pump—some words that occurred to us were

- hard
- work
- talking
- knees
- powerlessness
- fearful of rejection
- eyes closed

How does your list compare?

Next, ask yourself:

- What does my heart long to hear?

- What news do I want?

- What news do I need?

- What would bring me refreshment and renewal?

- What words can I use to express that in a new way?

- Would I dare use them?

- What positive words—good news words—would make the idea of prayer pleasant and something to be sought instead of endured? Make a list of them now.

KEEPING IT REAL

After you've composed your list, print it out and place copies of it in the places you usually pray. Then place copies in the places you'd like to pray:

- on the refrigerator door in the kitchen

- on the nightstand by your bed

- in your car (with your eyes open!)

Don't go with the "usual suspects"—church, Bible study and so forth. Look for new places to connect with God.

You might also want to try new ways of praying. What are ways that break you out of comfortable habits of posture and place and methods? Brent's friend Jenny Leiter does "e-prayers." When someone sends a prayer request via email, she does more than just shoot a quick prayer heavenward. She replies with a written email prayer. She types a prayer just for the person and then prays it out loud while asking the Holy to bless the person receiving it. Then she sends it.

The Prayer, Bless This Day

This day is full of beauty and adventure,

help me Lord to be fully alive to it all.

During this day, may I become a more thoughtful person,

a more prayerful person, a more generous and kindly person.

Help me not to be turned in on myself but

to be sensitive and helpful to others.

Let me do nothing today that will hurt anyone,

but let me help at least a little,

to make life more pleasant for those I meet.

When night comes, may I look back on this day without regrets;

and may nobody be unhappy because of anything

I have said or done or failed to do.

> Lord God, bless this day for me and all of us.
>
> Make it a day in which we grow a little more like your Son,
>
> and gentle as Mary His Mother.
>
> Amen.

Remember, part of learning a new way of praying is also learning to live into Paul's admonition to pray without ceasing. Sending an "e-prayer" is just one method of doing this. And it's handy since many of us spend a good deal of time in front of computer screens.

Jennie closes most of her one-on-one spiritual direction sessions with the question, "How would you like to be prayed for?" This question usually yields qualities that her clients would like to grow in themselves—courage, faithfulness, health, and so on. Occasionally, though, the answer is about the manner in which one wants to be prayed for. Every once in a while, a client looks surprised to hear that a prayer request would enter into a session. Jennie closes the session with a semi-crafted, almost-spontaneous, responsive vocal prayer that includes the client's answer to the question and also the threads of connection between the client and the Holy that have come to light in the conversation. Every session has different needs and metaphors. Every session therefore has different prayers.

Figuring out ways to include prayer in the flow of our daily activities helps us incorporate our interior spiritual life into our exterior activities. While that may sound easier said than done (and it is), the spiritual writer Thomas R. Kelly urges us to learn to meld our interior and exterior lives:

> How, then, shall we lay hold of that Life and Power, and live the life of prayer without ceasing? By quiet, persistent practice in turning all our being, day and night, in prayer and inward worship and surrender, towards Him who calls in the deeps of our souls. Mental habits of inward orientation must be established. An inner, secret turning to God can be made fairly steady, after weeks and months and years of practice and lapses and failures and returns. It is as simple an art as Brother Lawrence found it, but it may be long before we achieve any steadiness in the process. Begin now, as you read these words, as you sit in your chair, to offer your whole selves, utterly and in joyful abandon, in quiet, glad surrender to Him who is within. In secret ejaculations of praise, turn in humble wonder to the Light, faint though it may be. Keep contact with the outer world of sense and meanings. Here is no discipline in absentmindedness. Walk and talk and work and laugh with your friends. But behind the scenes keep up the life of simple prayer and inward worship. Keep it up throughout the day. Let inward prayer be your last act before

you fall asleep and the first act when you awake. And in time you will find, as did Brother Lawrence, that "those who have the gale of the Holy Spirit go forward even in sleep.

We invite you to, as Kelly said, "begin now, as you read these words, as you sit in your chair, to offer your whole selves, utterly and in joyful abandon, in quiet, glad surrender to Him who is within." Consider new ways that you can be in prayer while moving through your life.

GROWING NEW PRAYERS

We have found that an active prayer life, even as hard as it is to maintain at times, feeds and nourishes our interior lives. We want to grow into spiritual adulthood. To do so, we've discovered that we must put away some of those baby-food prayers that served us well as youngsters. It is okay for a child to pray, "God is great, God is good and we thank him for this food" or "Now I lay me down to sleep...." It is even okay for us to pray them. But if these prayers are the staple of our prayer life, then they ultimately keep us locked into a tiny revelation of God that is safe, comfortable and limited.

True, deep-hearted prayer opens us to our own hiddenness within. It is in going there that we can become aware of who God is and who we are. Sometimes our go-to prayers simply won't work in a new and challenging situation. So we must put them away and find more authentic prayers that fit.

Jennie had a client who was grieving her husband's suicide. They had been married over thirty years before he died. He had been depressed for the last five years, and while he was alive, she prayed for his recovery. She laid hands on him. She prayed for ease from his pain. She prayed for help for his deep emotional pain, and for them to have the closeness they once had in their relationship. None of these prayers seemed to help.

In the year after his death, the woman prayed for openings to know how she should be without her husband as a presence in her life. She prayed to stop grieving. She prayed she could forgive her husband for the depression and the choice to take his own life that made her so angry, and for the distance he created between them in the last years of their marriage. She believed that he grew to dislike and resent her because of his depression. She did not feel loved, or appreciated, though she continued to offer the best care to him that she could.

After months of prayer after his death, the woman came to a new understanding. It was difficult. She had shaped much of her adult life around addressing and meeting her husband's needs. In the last years before his death, she continued this caretaking in spite of the diminished emotional returns to herself. After his death, she felt called to throw off the caretaker role in her marriage, and in other areas of her life where she had taken it on. She gained strength. And then she shared that strength by beginning to express love to her children and others without trying to take care of their problems.

Her prayers and her loss opened her to an inner hunger for freedom. Through prayer she was able to embrace a new way of being in the world as that divinely-planted seed took root.

Prayer gives us time to focus our thoughts on the important things of life and faith. Prayer helps us connect with the God who desires to be known. Sometimes there are surprises to be uncovered along the way about what God is calling us to do or be. We change and grow until our very last breath. And as Evelyn Underhill says,

> Prayer means turning to Reality, taking our part, however humble, tentative, and half-understood, in the continual conversation, the communion, of our spirits with the Eternal Spirit; the acknowledgment of our entire dependence, which is yet the partly free dependence of the child. For Prayer is really our whole life toward God: our longing for Him, our "incurable God-sickness," as Barth calls it, our whole drive towards Him. It is the humble correspondence of the human spirit with the Sum of all Perfection, the Fountain of Life. No narrower definition than this is truly satisfactory, or covers all the ground.

Jennie's client had her worldview rocked first by her husband's illness and personality change. Then it was shaken by the disappointment of perceived unanswered prayers. It was further quaked by the shocking prayer-filled revelation that she was no longer to submit herself as chief caretaker and problem solver for others.

A way to open ourselves to new images is to start with comfortable prayers. Maybe even childhood prayers. We can use them as a springboard for new words and images. Singer-songwriter Carrie Newcomer did this when composing the song "Thank You, Good Night":

> Now I lay me down to sleep, into your care.
> Into my small hands, I'd clasp a prayer
> God bless my mom and God bless my dad
> God bless the best dog I've ever had
> Thank you, goodnight.
>
> All the things that have been done, have been
> done.
> All the things that have not been done, have not
> been done.
> And all the things that I'm sad and I'm glad I
> know,
> I'll breathe it out and I let it go.
> Thank you, Good night.
> In the glowing blue hour, the edges blur.
> But the more I live it seems the less I know for
> sure.

But before I close these day worn eyes,
I bow my head and breathe a sigh.
Thank you, goodnight.

Like a long exhale
Like a vapor trail
A wisp of a thing
That changes everything.

This place was once an ocean, a shallow sea.
We are the rightful heirs of an old story.
We are made of stardust fire and ice,
We are made of dreams, shadow and light.
Thank you, Goodnight.

EXERCISE 35—GROWING UP YOUR PRAYERS

In this exercise, you'll begin with a childhood or childlike prayer and enhance it to be able to reflect your adult life.

Take a prayer from childhood. It may be one of the familiar ones:

God is great! God is good!
Let us thank him for our food. Amen.

or

Bless us O Lord, and these thy gifts,
Which we are about to receive, from thy bounty,

Through Christ, Our Lord. Amen.

Or it may be one that comes entirely from your own prayer life. Use a prayer that has a feeling of being a lifelong prayer, something you have carried with you since you began praying. Use it as a springboard, much as Newcomer did with the familiar "Now I lay me down to sleep." Start with the first set of words. Instead of continuing with the usual ones that follow, be brave enough to see where your heart and mind take you in words. What cries to come after the safe and soothing words to represent where you are now?

Jennie grew up with this version of "God Is Great":

God is great! God is good!
Let us thank him for our food.
By his hands we all are fed.
Give us Lord our daily bread.

As she practiced this exercise it became:

God is great, God is good

Let us thank God for our food, and let us ask God about the ethics and economics of food.

What about the GMOs, Lord? What about animal cruelty and antibiotics? Are our hungers making trouble in the world? Am I right to thank you for the food, or should I sit in prayer over each greedy bit I take in, wondering what ripple effect

I am having on health and financial well-being for others? Lord, show me simplicity in my shopping and in my eating. Help me to be part of the solutions that will bring your way to earth through true stewardship of all that comes from you and true love for all of creation. Amen.

What a shift for a mealtime blessing! It reflects the complexity of food politics in the modern era. It also captures the thoughtfulness of going beyond saying "thank you." Especially saying thank you for something that may have been obtained at the horrible, life-choking expense of others. As you complete this exercise, notice what feels comfortable and continuous with your childhood prayer language and underlying ideas and what feels distinctly mature.

A SLIGHT CHANGE IN POINT OF VIEW

Another practice we can do to hear afresh the words we usually pray is to change a prayer slightly. You might be familiar with the Jesus Prayer—"Lord Jesus Christ, Son of God, have mercy on me, a sinner." This is not childhood prayer. It's a grown-up prayer full of spiritual implications (look at it through the lens of the three questions!). But it can be one of those prayers that become so much a part of our prayer lives that we breeze through it without hearing it.

Writer Jana Riess makes it new for her when she drops the "me" and inserts the name of someone she knows. "Lord Jesus Christ, Son of God, have mercy on Brent, a sinner." This slight but significant change turns the whole prayer around. For one, it names a friend as a sinner, which seems bold except for the fact that we all are. Still, we are not used to calling our loved ones sinners. And yet, the main point of the prayer is not about naming another as a sinner. Rather, it's the plea for mercy. Changing the Jesus Prayer in this way helps us see God as the dispenser of mercy. It brings to mind someone who needs our prayers. And it connects us as part of the incarnated body of Christ.

What prayers do you regularly use that could be slightly amended to help you hear the words afresh?

Another practice you can do is to take the prayers you use and reduce them to three words. Pare them to their essence. That's what spiritual writer Margaret Feinberg did for Lent one year. She did it because, as she writes:

> I realize how mindless I've become in my own prayer life. Yes, I feel free to express every desire, whim, ache and need to God—which is a good thing!—except that at times my prayers sound like a gushing four-year-old who talks in an eternal run on sentence. I realize that over time I've been increasingly unspecific and inattentive in my prayer life.

What three-word prayers would you construct to make prayer new? And to make it Good News?

There are many practices besides those above that you can do to enliven your prayer life and refresh your words and soul. Invite God to work with your holy imagination in making all things—including prayer—new. Invoke God's blessing to awaken the *imago Dei* in you so that you can be creative and responsive in prayer, as God is.

To pray is to take notice of the wonder, to regain a sense of the mystery that animates all beings, the divine margin in all attainments. Prayer is our humble answer to the inconceivable surprise of living. That's what Rabbi Abraham Joshua Heschel once wrote. Living the life of faith is one of inconceivable surprises—if, that is, we open ourselves to the possibility of inconceivability. Prayer helps us crack that door. Wonder. Mystery. Love. Grace. God. All are there. All are good news. All are new every day. Every moment. Prayer makes all things new—including our relationship with the great lover of our souls.

That is good news indeed. May your verbs always be active, your nouns from your soul, your adjectives and adverbs add beauty and depth, your difficult words be spoken with authenticity, and your prayer relationship with God be wise and deep and fulfilling.

> May these words of my mouth and this meditation
> of my heart
> be pleasing in your sight,

LORD, my Rock and my Redeemer. (Psalm 19:14)

APPENDIX 1

Exercises for Building Prayer as a Spiritual Practice

In "Beyond Words: Other Ways of Communicating—Or Not" (chapter eight), Jennie shared about resisting her daily practice. She found that when she yielded and returned to it, she felt God as the great physician who healed her from some old emotional trauma. Behind that story is the truth that sometimes it is just hard to get around to the daily practice, whether or not one is in a state of resistance, charged or not charged. Like any kind of lifestyle change, when you begin a practice of regular prayer, you are creating a new orientation and a new set of habits. If you are changing your diet or exercise routine, you need to accumulate some days of healthy eating or regular visits to the gym to begin seeing the benefits of the practice. Until you begin to see the fruit of your efforts, it may seem that willpower and commitment are the fuel in your tank. Finding the right practices can go a long way toward helping you stick with them until you can perceive the benefits of building a new habit. Here are some ideas for cultivating a daily prayer practice that will help you establish it as an integral part of your life.

1. Start a gratitude journal. Write a list of four or five things every day that you are thankful for. You might experiment with making your list first thing in the morning and then reviewing it before bed or making it at night and reviewing it in the morning. Jennie has found keeping a gratitude journal helpful because it allows her to look over weeks and months of entries to see the ebb and flow of her attention to different aspects of her life. You might want to bookend your gratitude entries, as Jennie often does, with "Dear God" (or some other salutation for the Holy) and "Love, Jennie" as a closing. Reading these entries aloud is a way to experiment with vocal prayer as well.

2. Light a candle. The simple gesture of bringing one's attention and intention to the practice of prayer can be a little ritual that brings you into the moment and increases your awareness of your relationship with God as it is in the present. One value of a prayer candle is that it's portable. When Jennie travels for work, she sometimes takes a candle with her. That way any hotel room or retreat center is transformed into a homey prayer place.

3. Use a prayer chair and prayer shawl. In the last fifteen years or so, many hospitals and churches have taken on knitting ministries in which crafters make prayer shawls for persons in times of illness and other hardship. The idea is that the knitters pray while they make the shawl and then the recipient of the shawl is wrapped in the prayers of another when she or he

wears the shawl. You could knit a shawl or simply have a scarf or other object that you set aside for your prayer practice. Though this idea of wearing something special for prayer may feel like a stretch if you are not into liturgy or ritual, having a "uniform" you don is a way of engaging intentionally in prayer. It serves as an outward reminder of the intention to practice. Similarly, having a chair or designated space in your house where you have your daily prayer time may help to make that space a reminder of the mind-and heart-set of prayer. When you sit in that chair or go to that place, you might find yourself better prepared to enter into your prayer practice.

4. Daily readers. What you take in through reading is similar to what you take in as food. One provides nourishment for body, the other nourishment for your mind. It is important to read things that inspire you. Consider beginning your daily prayer time with a short reading. There are Bible readers that help you read the entire Bible in 365 days. There are daily readers for 12-step programs, readers for women, Chicken Soup for the Soul readers and Lenten readers. Jennie has a long history of using daily readers for inspiration. Over time she has learned to be easy with herself concerning using them. She always has at least two, and usually three, readers by her chair. She also finds it important to rotate readers and to seek inspiration from the readings. Such readers are meant to be a tool, not a shackle. If one ceases to be stimulating, rest from it and be open to other

sources of inspiration. Sometimes a combination of reading and a little reflective writing in a journal, followed by prayer, can surface previously untended prayer and life topics.

APPENDIX 2

Prayer Exercises

Jennie has had success in workshops with offering fill-in-the-blank prayers like the ones in chapter three, so we thought we would include some more exercises like those to help get your juices flowing for crafted prayers. Below you will find exercises that include questions to stimulate your vocabulary and then a template for using the words on your list. You might consider this an ingredient-only recipe that comes without the measurements or mixing instructions. Don't let the limits of our imagination or the places where our words do not match your understandings be a stop to your creative prayers. Sometimes it is easier to begin not with a blank page but with something to edit nearer to the perfection of your heart's dialogue.

PRAYER FOR OTHERS (INTERCESSORY PRAYERS)

For many, the easiest times of prayer come as spontaneous, heart-felt prayers for loved ones or situations of sadness in the world. Take a moment to reflect on these questions:

• Who or what are you praying for?

- How are you feeling?

- What is the desired outcome?

- Are you able to release responsibility and control of the outcome to God? If not (or not just yet), then spend some time writing or thinking about what stands between you and surrender.

Now, write:

- Salutations for God that bring to mind that God takes care

- Verbs for what you hope God will do

- Emotions and thoughts that may prevent you from releasing this concern to God's care

And then fill in the blanks:

> Dear (Salutation for God),
>
> I am feeling (insert adjectives to describe how you feel in this moment about this topic). I ask for your attention and care for (insert name or descriptive phrase about the situation you are praying for). I really want (insert outcome), and I also want to trust that you will take care of things. I'm having a little trouble letting go of this worry, because I feel (insert more feelings about releasing concerns), so I also ask that you soothe me and help me to grow in trust.

Love,

(Insert your name)

PRAYERS IN TIMES OF DARKNESS

Times of despair are also times we can and should turn our hearts to God in prayer. Jennie's own experience has been that times of darkness have been times when she has not wanted to pray, mostly out of fear that nothing will change. In less dark times, she knows that something definitely will change in prayer—if nothing else, *she* will be changed by it.

Consider how you feel and whether or not a concrete external circumstance is causing your feelings. What hesitations might you have about turning to God in prayer at this time, whether it's because nothing will change or because it's a desire not to be seen in a state of darkness?

Now write:

- Salutations for God, especially ones that seem to be an antidote to the darkness, such as "Bringer of Light" or whatever comes to you.

- A list of emotions that are easy to acknowledge.

- A list of emotions that are harder to acknowledge. This list might be the things you hope no one notices.

Then fill in the blanks:

Dear (Salutation),

I feel (insert descriptors). Life seems very dark right now, and I'm not even sure I want to be having this conversation with you. I want to feel better. I'm looking to you to provide some ease, some comfort, some light, and nothing seems to be happening. In fact, I feel (insert difficult-to-acknowledge feeling words). As far as I can tell, I'm down because (is it circumstance or something else, or even unknown?). Can you please send a little light my way? This darkness seems too much to bear.

Love,

(Insert name)

PRAYERS THROUGH ANGER AND OTHER DIFFICULT EMOTIONS

Following the example of the Psalms, Jennie has developed a delight in prayers that include expressing anger and frustration. In many arenas, people, and especially women, are discouraged from showing any "negative" emotions. Through her experience praying the Psalms aloud (from beginning to the end of a psalm, not avoiding the violent entreaties to have enemies smote in one way or another), Jennie has found her anger lessened and her heart softened. Her heart opening has come from being able to feel and express her emotions uninhibited, and from an increased willingness to be seen as a whole person. Being angry or frustrated is part of the human experience, and our Creator knows this. Failing to acknowledge the difficult or "negative" emotions is a way of keeping ourselves from full participation in the holy conversation.

PRAYER IN ANGER

Consider: What you are angry about? Is it an old or recurring anger just boiling over, or is it a new anger? How do you feel about being angry? Are there any voices in your head offering discouragement about having or expressing your emotions?

Now write:

- Salutation for God.

- What are you angry about, in five words or less?

- How do you feel about being angry? (Okay? Uncomfortable?)

- What outcome do you want in the situation?

- What outcome do you want in yourself?

Fill in the blanks:

Dear (Salutation),

I am SOOOOOO angry. I don't understand why this is happening. Have you been paying attention? Do you know that (insert description about what's going on)? I want (insert your desired outcome for the situation). Can you help with that? Are you listening up there? Being angry is not pleasant for me. In fact, I feel (how you feel about being angry). I would like the situation to change, and I would like to feel change in me too. I want to (insert desired outcome in yourself). I don't feel like I deserve this, and your silence in the matter is making me doubt myself, and you too.

Looking forward to hearing from you,

(Insert name)

SURRENDER/POWERLESSNESS

After the anger, there is often a collapse into sadness and fear. The fire of anger yields to the steam of powerlessness. After all, if we could change the circumstance on our own, we might not even bother to pray. Twelve-step support groups have embraced a prayer that emphasizes surrender as a key to serenity. Here is another possibility.

Consider the variety of emotions you have experienced related to the situation you now bring into prayer and your response to being powerless or needing to surrender. Consider whether there is any part you have played in the circumstance.

Now write:

- Salutation for God (perhaps one that indicates an acknowledgment of power or authority)

- How you feel about the circumstance that brings you to a feeling of powerlessness or the need to surrender

- Some words to describe what you most deeply want

- Some words to describe what it would feel like to rely on something untrustworthy

- Some words to describe if you have played any part in the circumstance that you are struggling with

Fill in the blanks:

Dear (Salutation),

I am exhausted. I feel (insert feelings that bring you to surrender). I hate feeling powerless. Why did you make that part of being human? Ugh. I have no choice but to rely on you, and yet I'm worried that really (insert words about relying on something untrustworthy). And I'm afraid that somehow I brought this situation on myself by (insert words of self-responsibility). I really want (insert desire words). Can you help me with that, or at least help me want it less? I am so tired of all of this. Please help.

Love,

(Insert name)

GRATITUDE

One of the most formulaic occasions for prayer is the prayer before meals. Rarely do we hear prayers of gratitude except at mealtimes and sporting events. What would a prayer of gratitude look like if it came in your own words, in response to a sense of feeling blessed with more than food or a win?

Consider: What are you grateful for? What feels good in your life today, this week, this year? Can you remember a time when things weren't going so well? Consider what has dramatically improved since then?

Now write:

- Salutation for God

- Nouns—things you are grateful for

- Other feelings that go with gratitude

Fill in the blanks:

Dear (Salutation),

Wow. I am so thankful for (insert list). Beyond gratitude, I also feel (insert feelings). I wish I felt this way more often and that I remembered to talk with you about it all. Being grateful has made a big ripple in the rest of my life. I see the world differently when I have my gratitude glasses on. Can you help me remember that?

Love and gratitude,

(Name)

APPENDIX 3

Resources

While our book is primarily about language and prayer, we recognize that there are many other aspects to prayer. Learning the way of prayer is a lifelong enterprise. Below you'll find a list of books we think you might find helpful as you go deeper in your life of prayer. Some are classics and some are new—or will be new to you. They aren't one-size-fits-all, so not every recommendation may speak to you. Give them a chance though. Spend time with a book that gives you new images or ways of prayer and praying.

A Guidebook to Prayer: Twenty-Four Ways to Walk with God by MaryKate Morse (InterVarsity Press, 2013)—Focusing on the personalities of the Trinity, Morse offers twenty-four distinct types of prayer activities and exercises.

A Prayer Journal by Flannery O'Connor (Farrar, Straus and Giroux, 2013)—A glimpse at authentic praying from a master writer; O'Connor's prayers are raw, authentic and inspiring.

A Short and Easy Method of Prayer by Madame Guyon (www.ccel.org/ccel/guyon/prayer.titlepage.html)—A prayer classic!

Centering Prayer: Renewing an Ancient Christian Prayer Form by Basil Pennington (Image Books, 1982)—A book on reclaiming centering prayer, an ancient spiritual practice, for today's Christians.

Hearing God: Developing a Conversational Relationship with God by Dallas Willard (InterVarsity Press, 1984)—A classic with excellent advice on listening for God's voice.

How Then Shall We Live? Four Questions That Reveal the Beauty and Meaning of Our Lives by Wayne Muller (Bantam, 1997)—A book that poses four questions, similar in effect to the theological questions at the center of this book but more focused on knowing what we see and value in our own lives.

Men Pray: Voices of Strength, Faith, Healing, Hope and Courage by the editors of SkyLight Paths (SkyLight Paths Publishing, 2013)—An anthology of prayers and thoughts on prayer especially for men.

Prayer: Finding the Heart's True Home by Richard J. Foster (Harper-Collins, 1992)—A modern classic, filled with fresh images of prayer, especially how it connects our hearts with God's heart.

Prayer of Heart and Body: Meditation and Yoga as Christian Spiritual Practice by Thomas Ryan (Paulist Press, 2001)—For readers who enjoyed the taste of body prayer we offered and want to explore yoga and meditation, two increasingly popular embodied practices explored by this book by a Catholic priest.

Praying in Color: Drawing a New Path to God by Sybil MacBeth (Paraclete Press, 2007)—For those times when there are no words or you seem stuck with words, Sybil's book teaches you how to use the language of markers and crayons to connect with your soul and to craft fresh prayers from your heart.

Praying with Strangers: An Adventure of the Human Spirit by River Jordan (Berkeley, 2011)—We are all used to praying for people we love. What if we would pray for people we don't know? Not in the abstract (the starving children of...) but the strangers who come into our everyday lives at the grocery, drug store, hotel, and so on? That's what River Jordan did and it gave her both new prayer language and new experiences of prayer.

Primary Speech: A Psychology of Prayer by Ann and Barry Ulanov (Westminster John Knox Press, 1982)—A must-read for all students in the school of prayer. It covers a wide range of topics (fear, sexuality, fantasy, projection and more) and their relation to prayer.

Psalms for Praying: An Invitation to Wholeness by Nan Merrill (Continuum, 2007)—A faithful and faith-filled version of the prayerbook of the Jewish and Christian faiths. You'll find it helpful for developing new images of familiar Scriptures.

The Book of Awakening: Having the Life You Want by Being Present to the Life You Have by Mark Nepo (Conari Press, 2011)—Written by a Buddhist writer and poet, this book brings up many topics related to awareness of human nature and does not imply answers from the Christian worldview, therefore leaving room for readers to explore through their own lenses.

To Bless the Space Between Us: A Book of Blessings by John O'Donohue (Doubleday, 2008)—This is not a book on prayer; rather, it's a book of prayers. Blessings, specifically. And it is both a blessing and filled with examples of fresh prayer language.

Notes

CHAPTER 1: A NEW WAY TO PRAY

"If the only prayer you ever say": Meister Eckhart. Eckhart was a 12th century German philosopher and mystic.

"Please dear God, thank you for the amazing opportunities": Elaine Emmi is a Quaker and founding member of Utah Power and Light. This is from an email to Brent.

"God, please guide me, let faith fill my heart instead of fear": Jana Llewellyn is a writer and publisher of *The First Day,* an online and print journal of arts, culture, faith and practice (firstdaypress.org). This prayer is from an email to Brent.

CHAPTER 2: WHAT LIES BENEATH THE WORDS

The Prayer Before the Crucifix at San Damiano: www .ofm.org/francesco/pray/pray01.php.

"very dangerous business": Emilie Griffin, *Clinging: The Experience of Prayer* (San Francisco: Harper & Row, 1984).

Since this embedded theology is one of the main lenses: For a good explanation of the nuance of embedded and deliberative theology, see Howard W. Jones and James O. Duke's *How to Think Theologically* (Minneapolis: Fortress Press, 1996), especially the chapter titled "Faith, Understanding, and Reflection."

"To the Ground of All Being": Tom Rugh is a graduate of Colgate Rochester Crozer Divinity School and retired nonprofit executive. This is from an email to Brent.

"I praise the dance, for it frees people": *Lord of Creation: A Resource for Creative Celtic Spirituality,* ed. Brendan O'Malley (New York: Morehouse, 2008), p.43.

CHAPTER 3: GOD IN ACTION

"A childlike adult is not one whose development is arrested": Aldous Huxley, *Collected Essays* (New York: Harper & Row, 1958).

"Holy God, Holy Strong, Holy Immortal, have mercy on us": See http://en.wikipedia.org/wiki/Trisagion.

"Dearest Lord, teach me to be generous": *The Westminster Collection of Christian Prayers,* ed. Dorothy M. Stewart (Louisville: Westminster John Knox Press, 2002), p.315.

"Govern everything by your wisdom, O Lord": Quoted in Gregory Wolfe and Suzanne Wolfe, *Circle of Grace: Praying with—and for—Your Children* (New York: Ballantine Books, 2000), p.287.

"Grant that I may pass through the coming year": Howard Thurman, *Meditations of the Heart* (Boston: Beacon Press, 1953), p.96.

"In seeking the light": Ibid., p.96.

"Dear God, I am so afraid to open my clenched fists!": Henri J.M. Nouwen, *The Only Necessary Thing: Living a Prayerful Life* (New York: Crossroad, 1999).

"You will say, 'Christ saith this, and the apostles say this'": George Fox, *Journal,* Rufus Jones, ed. (Richmond, IN: Friends United Press, 1976).

CHAPTER 4: IMAGES OF AN ACTIVE-TENSE GOD

"God who in every land and every age": This prayer was adapted by Brent from a prayer by John S. Hoyland in Hoyland, *A Book of Prayers Written for an Indian College* (London: n.p., 1921), p.6.

"Sin boldly": Martin Luther, Letter to Philip Melanchthon, August 1, 1521, trans. Gottfried G. Krodel, in *Luther's Works,* vol.48 (Louisville: Fortress Press, 1963), p.282.

"Please include me in your work": By Karie Firoozmand in an email to Brent. Karie is the book review editor for *Friends Journal.*

CHAPTER 5: HOPE, BEAUTY AND DEPTH

That word is *epiousios:* Nicholas Ayo, *Give Us This Day Our Daily Bread: A Survey Theological and Literal* (South Bend, IN: University of Notre Dame Press, 1992), p.59.

"When you catch an adjective, kill it": Letter to D.W. Bowser on March 20, 1880. Available on twainquote s.com.

"Lord of the springtime, Father of flower, field and fruit": W.E.B. DuBois, *Prayers for Dark People* (Amherst: University of Massachusetts Press, 1980), p.6.

"Prayer is not doing, but being": Kathleen Norris, *Amazing Grace: A Vocabulary of Faith* (New York: Riverhead Books, 1998), p.351.

Church register picture: See http://sacredsandwich.co m/archives/9273.

"Lord, we JUST pray that you would JUST like, JUST really JUST totally": See www.acts17-11.com/pray_te ll.html.

"Our praying, however, needs to be pressed and pursued with an energy that never tires": Henry J. Chadwick, ed., *E.M. Bounds: The Classic Collection on Prayer* (Orlando, FL: Bridge-Logos Publishers, 2001), p.50.

"Watch, dear Lord, with those who wake": Quoted in *All Through the Night: Prayers and Readings from Dusk till Dawn,* ed. Michael Counsell (Louisville: Westminster John Knox Press, 2000), p.112.

"Please give me courage and confidence": Sarah R. Brown is director of operations at First Congregational Church in Burlington, Vermont. This is from an email to Brent.

"Pray as you can, not as you can't": Quoted in Melannie Svoboda, *Just Because: Prayer-Poems to Delight the Heart* (New London, CT: Twenty-Third Publications, 2010), p.72.

CHAPTER 6: UNPACKING MEANING

"concentrates the mind and enlarges the soul": Joan Chittister, *The Breath of the Soul: Reflections on Prayer* (New London, CT: Twenty-Third Publications, 2009), p.20.

"Eternal God, let thy spirit inspire and guide us":—a prayer by Pierre Ceresole, written in his last notebook while in prison for refusing to pay war-taxes. This translation was printed in *The Friend,* vol.104 (London: The Friend Publications Ltd, 1946), p.2.

"The outline for prayer that Jesus gives is simple": See http://inwardoutward.org/the-story/keep-on.

"The words we choose color the way we think and see": http://twitter.com/#!/kristatippett/status/31543 5900253401088.

"Holy Father hear our prayer": "The Lord's Prayer" by John Fischer, copyright 1969 Songs and Creations, Inc.

"O thou high and holy One!": Lady Deborah Castle Bowring, ed., *A Memorial Volume of Sacred Poetry by the Late Sir John Bowring* (London: Longmans, Green, Reader & Dyer, 1873), pp.163-64.

"Our Father which in heaven art": John Bunyan, *A Book for Boys and Girls: Or, Country Rhymes for Children* (London: Elliot Stock, 1889), pp.8-9.

"God, you'd better be with me in this!": Ashley Wilcox is an attorney and seminary student. This is from an email to Brent.

CHAPTER 7: JESUS, THE WORD OF GOD, AND OUR WORDS

"Without the incarnation, Christianity isn't even a very good story": Michael Spencer, *Mere Churchianity: Finding Your Way Back to Jesus-Shaped Spirituality* (Colorado Springs: Waterbook, 2010), pp.91-92.

"I ask for daily bread, but not for wealth": Inazo Nitobe was a Japanese Quaker. This prayer is from *Selections from Inazo Nitobe's Writings,* ed. Tadao Yanaihara (n.p.: 1936), p.159.

"on its highest level a new revelation of God": Rufus Jones, *Some Problems of Life* (Nashville: Cokesbury, 1937), p.192.

"The fact that God can be revealed in a personal life": Ibid., pp.196-97.

"Holy Trinity icon": See http://en.wikipedia.org/wiki/User:Andrei _Rublev.

"Jesus heal me (on intake of breath), Make me whole (on exhalation)": Catharine Phillips is a poet, spiritual director and Episcopal priest. Her writings can be found at http://allwillbewellperiod.blogspot.com. This prayer is from an email to Brent.

"Incarnational prayer may begin with the prayer of the lips": Ben Campbell Johnson, *To Will God's Will:*

Beginning the Journey (Louisville: Westminster Press, 1986), p.55.

"Jesus' idea is irresistible and irreversible": Ian McEwan, *Sweet Tooth* (New York: Random House, 2012), p.96.

CHAPTER 8: BEYOND WORDS

"Suscipe (Receive)": By St. Ignatius of Loyola. See www.loyolapress.com/suscipe-prayer-saint-ignatius-of-loyola.htm.

"Prayer, when it is real": Harry Emerson Fosdick, *Adventurous Religion and Other Essays* (New York: Harper & Brothers, 1926), p.75.

"This climate in which monastic prayer flowers": Thomas Merton, *Contemplative Prayer* (New York: Image Books, 1971), p.27.

"O Lord, baptize our hearts": See http://sojo.net/2013/03/07/prayer-of-the-day.

"In life, the process is often marked by a feeling of emptiness": Gerald G. May, *The Dark Night of the Soul: A Psychiatrist Explores the Connection Between Darkness and Spiritual Growth* (San Francisco: HarperCollins, 2004), p.136.

"True prayer is fulfilling the conditions": Fosdick, *Adventurous Religion,* p.86.

"As I have said": May, *Dark Night of the Soul,* p.135.

"Prayer heals": Henri Nouwen, *Show Me the Way: Readings for Each Day of Lent* (New York: Crossroad, 1996), p.86.

"The reason we can hope to find God": Rufus Jones, *Pathways to the Reality of God* (New York: Macmillian, 1931), pp. xi-xii.

CHAPTER 9: GOSPEL MEANS GOOD NEWS

"Oh, hold them, hold them": Cat Chapin-Bishop is an educator and long-time Quaker. This is from an email to Brent.

"One day, when I had been walking solitarily abroad": *The Journal of George Fox: A Revised Edition by John L. Nickalls* (London: Religious Society of Friends, 1975), p.15.

"How great is the power of Prayer! One could call it a Queen": Saint Thérèse of Lisieux, *Story of a Soul* (Washington, DC: ICS Publications, 1996), p.384.

"was generous with his pocket book, but not himself": William Hoffman, "The Question of Rain," in *God:*

Stories, ed. C. Michael Curtis (New York: Houghton Mifflin, 1998), p.95.

"God knows our needs": Ibid., p.96.

"This is the beauty of prayer and of Christian life": Oscar A. Romero, *The Violence of Love* (Maryknoll, NY: Orbis, 2004), pp.79-80.

"By contemplative prayer, I do not mean any abnormal": *Radiance: A Spiritual Memoir of Evelyn Underhill,* compiled and edited by Bernard Bangley (Brewster, MA: Paraclete, 2004), p.135.

"The Prayer, Bless This Day": See www.catholicdoors .com/prayers/english4/p02910.htm.

"How, then, shall we lay hold of that Life and Power": Thomas R. Kelly, *A Testament of Devotion* (San Francisco: HarperSanFrancisco, 1941), pp.11-12.

"Prayer means turning to Reality": Evelyn Underhill, *The Spiritual Life* (1937; reprint, Harrisburg, PA: Morehouse Publishing, 1985), p.61.

"Now I lay me down to sleep into your care": "Thank You, Good Night" by Carrie Newcomer, copyright 2013, Windchime Productions.

"Lord Jesus Christ, Son of God, have mercy on me, a sinner": www.orthodoxchristian.info/pages/Jprayer. html.

"I realize how mindless I've become in my own prayer life": http://margaretfeinberg.com/why-im-giving-up-prayer-for-lent.

To pray is to take notice of the wonder: Abraham Joshua Heschel, "The Holy Dimension" in Susan Heschel, ed., *Moral Grandeur and Spiritual Audacity: Essays* (New York: Farrar, Straus and Giroux, 1996), p.341.

Acknowledgments

That you are holding this book in your hand is evidence of the many hands and hearts that made it possible. We are grateful to the owners of those hands and hearts for carrying us as we carried this book into being. Prayer is absolutely common, and yet we found that talking about it, examining it and changing the way we do it is not at all common. A broad thank you is due to all the people who were willing to do just that with us, from attendees in the very earliest workshops Jennie led on this topic to friends and colleagues who asked either of us what we were working on and didn't walk away when the conversation suddenly went deep into the heart of prayer.

We are grateful to InterVarsity Press for saying yes to our proposal, and for saying "yes" and "yes, but..." as we progressed through the manuscript. Cindy Bunch, our editor, pushed us graciously in ways that made this book better than it would have been.

All those who have prayed aloud within our earshot or have been with us when we prayed aloud deserve special thanks for their willingness to be seen and to see us as we took sometimes awkward steps toward authenticity in prayer. We learned so much from you.

Brent is grateful, as always, for Nancy's support for his writing, encouragement along our pilgrim way, her deep spirituality and her loving-kindness over the years. He's also deeply appreciative of the Friends at West Newton Friends Meeting in Indianapolis, Indiana, who hold him in prayer as he travels in ministry and who seem to enjoy and learn from the Sunday school classes he offers. He's thankful to the many friends (some of whom are Friends) who encouraged him through conversations about spirituality and through prayer and offered glimpses of their own prayer lives. Some of these special friends include Aaron Spiegel, Barry Crossno, Betsy Blake, Carrie Newcomer, Deborah Fisch, Laura Melly and Shannon Isaacs. Some other friends, including Ashley Wilcox, Cat Chapin-Bishop, Catharine Phillips, Elaine Emmi, Jana Llewellyn, Karie Firoozmand, Sarah Rejoice Brown and Tom Rugh, shared prayers that are important to them.

Jennie is deeply grateful for Newell, her beloved husband and life partner, whose own deep journey with prayer and skill with language and metaphor feed their conversations on a daily basis, taking her to new edges of wonder and faithfulness. She is also grateful for Woolman Hill Quaker Retreat Center in Deerfield, Massachusetts, where much of this book was written as she and Newell served there as Friends in Residence. She offers thanks for the Quakers who fueled her clarity about the importance of prayer and of the conversations we have (or don't have) in our communities about God and our relationship with God. Most central in her heart among these are the members of Clear Creek Monthly Meeting in Richmond,

Indiana, her friends at Earlham School of Religion, and those Quakers in Roanoke Monthly Meeting in Virginia who helped her understand her call to ministry. Closer encouragement still came from friends at Mt. Toby Quaker Meeting in Leverett, Massachusetts: Margaret, Jill, Jim, Dorrie, Victoria, David, Alan, Mary Ellen, John and "the usual suspects" at midweek meeting for worship who were her prayer companions at the end of many writing days.

For all of you, we lift a prayer of thanksgiving.

Seeking and Finding God in the Verbs—the Workshop

Jennie developed this workshop in answer to her sense that many worshiping communities do not foster opportunities for their members to speak about their relationship with God beyond the use of formulaic prayers and confessions of faith. Many words used in churches have an insider quality that implies that the insiders know the meaning of the words intimately. Yet a hunger remains among individuals for a closer intimacy and authenticity with God. This use of "short-cut" words in churches that lack full-color meanings bleeds into personal prayer life. Such prayer often leaves people praying inauthentically and not finding depth in their relationship with God.

Before she created the workshop, while working on a project related to helping congregations learn to name and nurture gifts for leadership, Jennie realized that the work of discernment is not possible in a community without trust and a common sense of what is at the center of the discernment process. If a community is not able to speak about God, then speaking about God's will for the community or for a person in the community is not possible. Many members of worshiping communities do not speak about God with one another. This is a block to discernment.

The Seeking and Finding God in the Verbs workshop addresses both issues. It creates a container for discussion of individuals' relationships with God while also fostering community conversation about shared glimpses of the Holy. When communities want to do corporate or shared discernment around God's will, they must have a shared vocabulary of faith in order for basic communication to happen. Encouraging individuals to have a relationship with the Holy, and to speak of it, strengthens the individuals and the community. It also brings about awareness of the complexity that faith communities live in. There is that simplicity on the other side of complexity that brings inner freedom.

Some of the exercises in this book are taken directly from those early versions of the workshop. Others have been added in successive offerings. Since its beginning, the workshop has varied in length from ninety minutes to twenty hours over the course of five days. The best effects of the workshop, which we hope have transferred to the book, include playful delight and self-discovery, as well as ease in talking with others about things often not discussed.

Illuminating the lenses we each wear and taking them off for closer inspection requires a feeling of safety and also a container of encouragement. The workshop encourages both.

For information on the workshop, visit Jennie at www .jennieisbell.com.

About Jennie

Jennie's call to ministry is about accompanying people (and sometimes groups) as they tune their minds, hearts and bodies to perceive and respond to glimpses of the Holy in-breaking. She provides one-on-one spiritual direction sessions in person and by phone, and regularly serves faith communities as a retreat and workshop leader. In addition to the workshop that started this book, Seeking and Finding God in the Verbs, other topics for her offerings include

- Faith and Philanthropy: Connecting Vision to Funding, a program that helps faith communities discover the connection between mission and money and develop passion for fundraising

- Gifts in the Body: Living into Corporate Discernment, a program that creates a culture of naming and nurturing gifts in the congregation as a way to identify and fulfill the divine calling of a given community

- Spirituality in/and the Body, a program that brings the body back into the life of faith, from body prayers and laying on of hands to the historic study of healing in our tradition; a program of healing into wholeness for any who have suffered a mind-body split in an effort to be "good"

For more information about Jennie's teaching and spiritual direction ministries, visit www.jennieisbell.com or email her at jennieisbell@gmail.com.

About Brent

In addition to his ministry of writing, Brent also enjoys a ministry of leading workshops and speaking. Some of his most popular workshops are

- The Sacred Compass: Spiritual Practices for Discernment, a workshop for those who want to learn discernment as a life-process

- Writing from the Heart: Telling Your Soul's Stories, for those who want to unlock their spiritual stories

- Awaken Your Senses (with Beth Booram), geared toward helping people experience God in new ways by using their bodies and souls

- Being Quiet: The Practice of Holy Silence, based on Quaker silence, teaches how to be quiet and still in our souls amidst the clamor of everyday life

If you would like more information about Brent's writing, his spirituality workshops and retreats, or would like to contact him about other speaking engagements, you can reach him through his website at www.brentbill.com or via email at brentbil@brentbill.com.

You can read new material and see photography by Brent at holyordinary.blogspot.com.

formatio

TRADITION. EXPERIENCE.
TRANSFORMATION.

Formatio books from InterVarsity Press follow the rich tradition of the church in the journey of spiritual formation. These books are not merely about being informed, but about being transformed by Christ and conformed to his image. Formatio stands in InterVarsity Press's evangelical publishing tradition by integrating God's Word with spiritual practice and by prompting readers to move from inward change to outward witness. InterVarsity Press uses the chambered nautilus for Formatio, a symbol of spiritual formation because of its continual spiral journey outward as it moves from its center. We believe that each of us is made with a deep desire to be in God's presence. Formatio books help us to fulfill our deepest desires and to become our true selves in light of God's grace.

Made in United States
North Haven, CT
10 October 2022

25258607R00137